G000156010

TREVOR TANNER

TRUE STORIES FROM THE FRONTLINE
OF TOTTENHAM'S STAUNCHEST FANS

JOHN BLAKE

Published by John Blake Publishing Ltd,
3 Bramber Court, 2 Bramber Road,
London W14 9PB, England

www.johnblakepublishing.co.uk

First published in paperback in 2010

ISBN: 978-1-84454-730-2

All rights reserved. No part of this publication may be reproduced, stored in a
retrieval system, or in any form or by any means, without the prior permission in
writing of the publisher, nor be otherwise circulated in any form of binding or cover
other than that in which it is published and without a similar condition including
this condition being imposed on the subsequent publisher.

British Library Cataloguing-in-Publication Data:

A catalogue record for this book is available from the British Library.

Design by www.envydesign.co.uk

Printed in Great Britain by CPI William Clowes Ltd, Beccles NR34 7TL

1 3 5 7 9 10 8 6 4 2

© Text copyright 2010 Trevor Tanner

Papers used by John Blake Publishing are natural, recyclable products made from
wood grown in sustainable forests. The manufacturing processes conform to the
environmental regulations of the country of origin

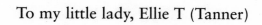

To my little lady, Ellie T (Tanner)

CONTENTS

INTRODUCTION

I actually thought that I had finished this book but obviously not.

On a recent visit to my publisher to go through the formalities of finishing a book I was pleasantly surprised to hear that my first book had done so well. After all the struggles to get this book together it's strange because those few words seemed to make it all worthwhile.

He was honest with me and said that although they thought that the book would do well they were taken aback at the sales. They were expecting good sales when it first came out, but thought it would just tail off like most books of this genre do!

Obviously I said, 'I'm more than pleased to hear that, as it's my book, but all the credit must go to our firm as a whole.' People out there must have wanted this book whatever team they supported, which I knew would and hoped would be the case.

The book I'm talking about is *Tottenham Massive* and I am Trevor Tanner, the author of that bestselling book. *Tottenham Massive* charts my years running the Spurs firm, yid army, whatever you want to call it, starting at the beginning some 20-odd years ago,

The first book was the start of an epic adventure to get us respected as the football firm of the '90s and new millennium. The fruits of this first came to mind when I was a 19-year-old striving to take Spurs onto another level, to have us recognised in the same breath as the Millwalls, West Ham and the Chelseas of that era.

Growing up in south-east London only proved to make me even more determined. I wanted what they had back then and some more. The easiest thing in the world would have been for me to go to my local club Millwall and join the rest of the loons!

But that was never an option with me. Spurs was my team. Always was and always will be! So with a few friends who I go back 20-odd years with now, we took Spurs to the top of our world, culminating in a three-year prison sentence for yours truly.

Way back in the day I was serving in the merchant navy, travelling all over the world, a job I loved and to this day I regret leaving so early, but that's life and you have to move forward. I was just too young to appreciate it and so focused on taking us to the top that something had to give and this time it was my dream job, although more would follow – not as glamorous, I grant you, but jobs all the same. Ie; Royal Mail (sacked because I got bit by a police dog – which got a medal!) and in fairness I wouldn't work Saturdays! British Rail: let go reluctantly because I received three years (fair enough). And the Rail again: which I left because it was by now privatised and a shit job.

The first book charts our rise and rise to the top of the ladder with our despised rivals, Chelsea, and our battles with Millwall, West Ham, Leeds Utd, Boro and Man United. It also focuses on our growing following and reputation on the England scene and of course our travels as a firm in Europe. The first book is a bit of a boy's own adventure, going out and doing what you set out to do!

This brings me up to this book, which is the natural sequel to the first one. This book charts where we finished off, where we all are today! Which has meant prison for a few of the boys and numerous banning orders handed out and although they are a deterrent in one way they are also totally out of order, the way they are handed out and not always to the right people! And like everything there are ways to get around this if you're determined enough!

I escaped prison myself by the skin of my teeth and some months on the run, which is detailed inside. This book is quite a bit more personal than the first. I want to give the reader an idea what it's like to suddenly have to change your lifestyle drastically, to stand on your own two feet if you like, to convert that same buzz and passion to the real world without breaking the law. For a while it feels as if the party is going on without you but, ironically, I've probably had more rows outside football, which in a way I suppose was inevitable, but sad really.

This is about the firm at the top of their game and having to watch a lot of it from the sidelines – all this I go into detail later. It eventually leads me up to the time that I can rejoin the boys and in which direction I am now going to go.

It charts the brutality that Spurs and Chelsea are still capable of and highlights the growing hostility with West Ham in particular. I want this book to show people that we are nothing like the feral hoodie scum that plague our streets, preying on weak targets. We only hurt each other – or other firms, I should say. People may think that is a cliche, but it's true. That's a fact, it's like all youth culture, the people may change and so may the clobber, but whatever happens it's always there and so football violence will always be there in some form or another and that's a fact. The authorities know it, but won't admit it and the Premier League can bang on about it being the best league in the world but whether they like it or not it will always be there under the surface.

It hasn't been easy to write this second book but then nothing in life that's worth doing ever is. I have had distractions from all over the place from people who should know better, even from people who are my own, which is sad, but as a good friend of mine likes to remind me – if people don't like the book tell 'em to go and write their own fucking book!

This book will also focus on the growing power of our youth firm and go into more detail on my private life than the first book did, something I might add I'm not all together comfortable with, but that's a price you have to pay to a certain extent.

Writing a book is like going on a personal journey of discovery and taking a few people along for the ride. Anyone with half a brain should at the very least respect the effort that it takes to put a book out there, whatever the subject is.

This is a rollercoaster ride of thrills and spills, it's about Spurs' firm at the top of their game, it's about everyday life. Spurs are a closed firm which makes them special as – believe me – you would have to go a long way to find a better group of people in the country. We can rip another firm apart on our day if needs be, but also we know how to have a good time and it's been my pleasure to lead this little firm for so long and whatever path I decide to take, I shall have memories to last me a lifetime.

I have a beautiful little girl who is, scarily, now nine and is growing into a beautiful little person! A beautiful fiancée, pals that would go to the ends of the earth for each other. In other words (where did it all go wrong?), this is my story, *our* story.

The jealousy and back-stabbing that I have had to endure this time around, and made this second one so hard to write, is now in the past. It makes this book even more of an achievement. I can honestly say that I haven't deliberately set out to upset anyone with this book and I couldn't give two fucks if you believe that or not! I've just told it how it is.

If I've had a pop back at anyone either in this book or on the street it's because they deserve it and deep down people know that this is a proper true book, not one of your Chelsea, West Ham fantasy tales and that's not being arrogant or disrespectful, just the truth.

People were obviously crying out for something different, something real, something true, something brutal, a true account of our world from someone proper! Whatever walk of life you come from – girls, boys, firms – whatever your allegiance, sit back and enjoy my exploits running the best firm in the country at this moment in time. Yid army forever!

Anyone who has helped me to put this together, in any shape or form (and probably been driven mad) then thank you from the heart! That's your lot – read on!

Trevor Tanner

CHAPTER 1
ON THE RUN – WAS IT FUN?

I remember one time, when my missus was driving down from Portsmouth with me and I had to sign on again. It was starting to get to us by now. It was getting a bit ridiculous – every time I saw a copper in the street I nearly jumped out of my skin! Silly, I know, but that's how it gets to you. This was having an effect on both of us now, which is natural. People are just not designed to live under this sort of sustained pressure.

I knew something had to give, and I didn't want it to be this relationship. In the back of my mind, I knew I had to hand myself in.

At Bromley, I waltzed in and out again, albeit with my heart rate going through the roof. This ain't too healthy, I thought to myself. Me and my girl had to stay at hotels, just up the road from where I actually lived, which at first was quite a buzz. A bit naughty, a bit Bonnie and Clyde.

But that soon wore off. The thing that really brought it home was the Old Bill circling the house every couple of hours and banging on the door. This wasn't right. My girl was really scared they would burst in when we were there, which would have caused untold dramas.

They did do a very naughty move, though, and they know it! They were having no joy with the ordinary plod, so, in their wisdom, they chose to send the Flying Squad down the hill! Can you believe it? It was now getting fucking ridiculous. They actually broke in the back door and climbed through a window to leave a note on the table.

'Hand yourself in, Trevor!'

Can you believe that? I should've sued their arses big time, the cheeky fuckers. So it was happy days all round!

I remember one time when the missus and I were driving around the corner from my house and there were actually Old Bill going through the front door. It was crazy, and it was making my girl a bag of nerves. Me, too, to be honest. The thrill of the hunt had well and truly worn off, that was for sure. We drove back up the road to the hotel we were staying in, if you can call it a hotel. It was like something out of *Fawlty Towers*, except that it wasn't funny. It was just full of assorted weirdos. It was time to make the call.

I went outside on to the forecourt and phoned my brief and friend, Ola. He told me straight: it was a fuckup. No one likes being told that, but, whether I liked it or not, it was what I needed.

I don't know how, but he managed to call off the dogs. (Ola's words, not mine. Perfectly apt, though, I thought!) He managed to buy me the weekend with my girl and put his arse on the line by saying to the Old Bill that we would both be there on the Monday morning.

I tried to enjoy the weekend, as much as you can with a warrant hanging over you and the thought of being remanded on the Monday! We stayed in a nice little hotel and had a drink at a lovely little boozer overlooking the harbour, which to me, coming from south London, is paradise. I find it really therapeutic watching all the boats drift by, and it's even better with a pint in your hand.

I love it in the winter as much as the summer, sitting inside with a fire going, watching the waves crashing outside the window. They're all used to it down there and think it's hilarious that I love it so much. But I don't care: it's all good-natured. If they were staring at tower blocks all day, they would understand. For those few hours, it just stopped the world a little bit. You really can't buy those moments. I didn't want to be anywhere near London: it would have just been a constant reminder of what I had to face.

The grassing slags – or, I should say, slags who go in the

Paxton Arms, Crystal Palace; you know who you are – were causing me and my nearest and dearest untold grief and there really was no need for it. That landlord had only been in the boozer a few weeks and was barring everyone (so you get the picture). I remember he even barred my ex's father.

I fucking hate him for what he did, and what he put me and my fiancée and family through. A proper scumbag. He had enough chances to withdraw his statement but would have none of it. The thing that amazes me more than anything was the way that people I knew well carried on drinking there as if nothing had happened. You really do find out who your friends are in this kind of situation, that's for sure.

Another landlord, who has a well-known boozer by Palace's ground, tried to reason with him and told him that it was pointless what he was doing. But, again, the prick wouldn't have it. (This was all done without my knowledge, of course!)

CUT ADRIFT

During my enforced exile from Spurs and because of the banning order I was on – which said I wasn't allowed at any train stations or licensed premises in central London (what a fucking joke!) – I was only left with my little part of south London, or I could go *outside* London. You couldn't make it up!

So, if Palace were at home on a Saturday evening, I would slip over there in the evening to have a laugh and a few beers with the boys. Also, it was just nice to be part of a football environment again. Something I was missing bad. I suppose I was lonely really. I had been cut adrift from my own boys, who were all doing their own thing over there. It did piss me off that more of them didn't come over to see me, and I won't forget it! But I guess that's just human nature: out of sight, out of mind. And to get anyone to come to south London was like pulling up trees – fucking hard work. So, as Palace was only a few miles away and I had known all the boys for years, it was only natural that I would slip over there for a beer now and again. It was either that or just sit at home alone (happy days).

We had a few laughs and a few rows. One came one evening after a home game. I think it was against Charlton, and everyone knows that these two firms don't like each other, to put it mildly. So we found a little backstreet boozer, a proper shithole. Plastic glasses all round. This was well after the game had ended, about half past nine, I guess. It was just me and a few top boys who I had been pals with for years. There were a couple of Jocks down with them who go to the matches with them every now and again; they were Celtic bods.

For some reason, they were more interested in me at first. They were fine and I was patient and polite, as, at the end of the day, even though I only lived down the road, it wasn't my team or my firm, so I was a guest really. One of them in particular started to really get on my fucking nerves with his constant barrage of questions. You know what I mean. We've all been caught with boring cunts like that in a boozer, who just keep yapping away, convinced that everyone is enjoying *their* conversation.

'Do you know so-and-so?'

No, you silly cunt, it was only *my firm*! The funny thing was, the bod he was going on about is a silly fat twat who I'm sure I have given a dig at one time.

Then it got round to Aberdeen. The final straw, though, was when he started getting on his mobile and asking questions, trying to get me on the phone to talk to fucking strangers. By this time I could have quite happily stuck the phone up his arse! I started to think that he could be Old Bill the way he was going on. Unfortunately, that's one of the side effects of the paranoid, insular world that football bods inhabit. And I have seen geezers, mostly innocent, getting battered because the 'word' is they are Old Bill. In reality, they are just busy bastards making a nuisance of themselves, and trying desperately to get in with everyone, being someone they are really not. Then all it takes is someone with a bit of respect to cop the hump with the poor bastard and it's not a pretty sight, trust me.

I remember years ago, when we were coming back from

an away game, and one of the boys who had not long joined up with the firm was raising such suspicions. The adrenalin, testosterone, booze, charlie, whatever, was well flowing in the air, as it normally does on a naughty trip up North. And this geezer, who I won't name, for some reason thinks he is a right chap now. Personally, I can't stand the prick any more. Anyway, he was going to get it big time. I stepped in and told the boys to fuck off and leave him alone, thus saving him from getting a good hiding! I should've let them carry on thinking about it, but I don't like bullies.

Obviously, there are untold grasses at football, and I have my suspicions, as does everyone else. I'm not saying it's big or clever getting nicked, because it's not (OK, kids?). But, if you are involved in our game, then the law of averages says sooner or later you are going to get a tug. So, naturally, you're always going to be suspicious of someone who goes all over the country, Europe, wherever, getting involved and never getting tugged. Whether that is right or wrong, I don't know! Some people are just lucky, I guess (I certainly wasn't), and, among us, there's no doubt that there are genuine grasses.

But, let's face it, there are a million ways now that they can get their information to the plods. First it was mobiles, and now you have these sad cunts on the Internet all fucking day, which has got to be one of the biggest tools the plods have. So the chances of the sneaky fuckers getting caught out are near impossible. As far as I'm concerned, the Old Bill really do have it locked down nowadays.

Anyway, back in the boozer. This geezer really was a prick and wouldn't shut up. I actually moved away from him. As I said earlier, it really wasn't my fight; I was a guest. But my patience was wearing thin. So what does the fool do? Yes, you guessed it: he gets even closer to me.

Standing near me was another Jock who goes with Palace; I'll call him G. He's as good as gold and game as you like. I saw him one day in the street, and, though there's all the animosity going on, he greeted me with a smile and a handshake. As always, he is his own man.

Anyway, I could tell he didn't like the pair of them, as he totally blanked them and kept to himself. Then all of a sudden, hell broke loose. *Bang!* G smacks the irritating little cunt in the mouth. Fuck it, I'm having some of this! Suddenly I'm trading punches with him toe to toe. It was a proper little row. G was still having it and so was one of the other top boys. Once I saw one of them go down, I knew he had had enough.

It was an awkward one, and the boys who knew them were trying to intervene. I've seen so many of these situations get really ugly, so G and I fucked off to another pub. And that was that, apart from a bit of moaning. Well, he should've kept his mouth shut. Oh, and G was a Rangers fan.

A DUST-UP IN THE GARDEN

So I'd still got this monkey on my back – it's weird how things go. Every other aspect of my life was going well. I had not long started seeing a great sort (that's slang for woman, by the way) – the one I'm still with. I had a few quid. Things were OK apart from the thought of an impending court case. And, as always, the very great threat of prison hangs over you like a dark cloud, and, unless you're not the full ticket, it'll always be creeping into your mind at various times during the day, and especially at night.

I think it's true what they say: problems feel much worse at night, especially on freezing-cold, pitch-black nights in southeast London! I know it's all psychological, but I can totally understand what people are getting at. Somehow, I can't see these problems looking as bad in the Algarve on a warm summer's night, unless you are off your nut and jump on a 180mph motorbike!

One night I was in a boozer, right in the shadow of Palace's main station. It was a typical south London boozer: bit of music, various characters, a few sorts. Palace weren't at home this evening, and I had just gone for a drink to meet up with a few of the boys. It was a Saturday night and a pal of mine was bringing down a couple of fellas he knew to try to help me with my situation. One of them was about seven foot tall – I kid you not – and built like a brick shithouse. The other one

9

was shorter, bit under my height but stocky, and I knew straight away I was going to have grief with him. Don't ask me how – it's just instinct that's born into you after years of living on your nerves. The way he looked at me when he walked in said it all. He looked straight through me. I knew immediately that he was fucking Chelsea. But they were also definitely a couple of pikeys.

The big lump was OK and we settled down to chatting business and having a bit of banter. I wouldn't have trusted him as far as I could throw him, though, and that wouldn't be fun, that's for sure! But the short fucker was just hovering around and generally being a fucking nuisance making silly comments and what have you. I just kept trying to ignore him the best I could, but you could feel the tension in the air. It really was that edgy.

Then, for a while, things settled down again and I was even having a bit of a chat with the geezer. But fuck knows what he was on! The big lump he had brought with him just ignored him. Fucking great! I really needed this.

There were a few Palace boys in the boozer sitting right behind me, so I knew everything would be good. Then, out of the blue, while I was in conversation, he came over and gave it the large!

'Me and you best go outside,' he said, like something out of a bad Western. I thought he was on a wind-up.

'You must be fucking joking,' I said. But he wasn't. This is what the little cunt came for, that's for sure. I looked behind me and nobody moved. I was surprised, I must admit – not that I expected them to jump all over him, even though the prick deserved it. But it's nice to know you have some backup. I spotted one of my mates' birds sitting there. She couldn't believe it and was well pissed off with their reaction. So I was on my own.

'Come on, then, you mouthy cunt!' I said. 'Let's go in the garden.'

The last thing I needed was another row in the boozer – then I *would* be well and truly fucked. So me, the psycho and the big lump – and nobody else – went into the garden which was more like a concrete, sunken arena, pitch black, with a couple of shitty chairs, like something out of the film *Fight Club*. It was surreal; I couldn't believe it was happening, but it was, and I had to deal with it. I think I was in shock at the fact that these two had come to give me a beating. I somehow went on autopilot, as you tend to do if you have been in a few rows, which, let's face it, I have.

The thing I will always remember is that the phone rang, and it was my missus down in 'Pompey'. For some reason, I hadn't gone down there that weekend. Instead, I'd told her to go out with her mates and I would see her the following weekend.

I must be fucking mad! I thought to myself. I could have been down at the seaside on the piss with my girl. Instead, I was in a concrete bunker in the backstreets of southeast London having to deal with two psychos! She was all merry and asked if I was OK.

'Yeah, I'm fine,' I said. 'I've just got a small problem to deal with. I'll ring you back.'

All the time, the loony was just staring at me with a puzzled look on his boat while the gorilla was hovering beside me. For a split second I thought, Are they both gonna jump me?

No time to think. Autopilot kicked in big time. Without thinking, I threw a right hand straight into his mouth. He came back at me with a flurry of punches to my head and body. But they weren't doing any real damage. I had busted his hooter and there was claret everywhere. Also, as I was taller, I managed to get him into a headlock and restrict his movement, but he was awkward and clearly fucking radio! I threw a couple more and he was still going. Whatever the little prick was on had made him even stronger. He was cut to pieces, though, and I was covered in his claret.

The big lump, his pal, who was watching all this, must have decided he had had enough, which he had (there was no need for it, after all), but he had only himself to blame. The fucking idiot, though, the smaller guy, was having none of it, and, to my amusement, his pal gave him a dig as well, which well confused me. But fuck him! He had called it on and got exactly what he deserved. And, if his pal wanted to give him a dig, then so be it! Sounds harsh, but this ain't Queensberry Rules: it's street fighting at the back of a boozer, in the pitch dark, in the middle of winter, with two mental pikeys who could have pulled out anything on me! So I'll take a bit of help any time, even if it was a surprise source.

I walked back in the boozer and everyone was all over me (a bit bloody late). I sat down next to my pal's missus, and she told me how embarrassed she was that none of them had come with me, when she could see what was going to happen before I even went outside with the mouthy little mug. But it had all been over in minutes, and I'm not saying for a moment that the bods I knew would want to see me hurt (at least I hope not), as I had known some of them for years. I know, though, that there were a few embarrassed looks when they saw the claret all over me, and then muggy bollocks appeared through the door with his nose hanging off.

And then everyone wants to know! But I was having none of it. I was more concerned about the Old Bill showing up. Even though I had done fuck all wrong, it was the last thing I needed, especially sitting covered in another bod's gore. And, unbelievably, I had heard rumours that the geezer wanted the plods involved. You couldn't make it up! The landlord of the boozer was as good as gold, though.

We had a few beers, but nothing major. I had only come out for a quiet night to just get out of the house. As I said, why I never went to Pompey with my missus I'll never know! But life's funny like that. It's all about decisions, and making calls can change things at the drop of a hat. (Thank fuck I never let them help me out with my little problem!)

It was a crazy few months – or should I say days? I had another just up the road a few weeks after this incident, when me and a few of my Palace boys went to visit a crazy Irish bar where we knew the guvnor, who happened to be a Spurs fan as well, believe it or not.

It was a real sawdust-on-the-floor place, Paddies, pikeys and locals all mixed together, but I have to say I was treated only with kindness and respect in there. We had some great nights in there with their mad foot-stomping bands and, amazingly, you got a few lovely little sorts in there as well. Not that it was any good to me, since I was taken, but it made for a nice atmosphere on certain nights. It wasn't for me all the time, since it was well hectic and attracted some right loons, but I had a pal who loved it so I would tag along now and again.

I remember one night how a group of local gyppos, travellers, whatever you want to call them, walked in, all with dogs and goats and God knows what else. The guvnor knew them but I could tell they were going to be a pain in the arse. To cut a long story short, they did play up and didn't want to leave, so we backed the guvnor up and after a little bit of drama and a few words they fucked off. He never forgot that, though.

I had enough though, so I thought, Let's go round the corner to another boozer – which happened to have a big Spurs flag behind the jump. As we were walking round the corner, we went past this big black geezer with dreads having a toe-to-toe row with a woman holding a baby at a bus stop. My pal went, 'Look at that, what a cunt! That's bang out of order.'

And it was, but was it his bird? A complete stranger? Or what? He was obviously high on something.

The next thing we knew, he punched the bird full in the face while she was still holding the baby. Fuck this! Why me? I thought. Of all the times and places to be! Why now? Why this? Why me? I had to do something. It just wouldn't be right not to. If I woke up in the morning and read about this loony in the paper, I wouldn't forgive myself. And everyone was just standing there doing fuck all, so I ran for him and got him in a headlock and told him to calm the fuck down before he got nicked or hurt the bird beyond repair. But he was having none of it and started throwing punches like a wildman.

I didn't need this, trading punches with a big geezer at a bus stop. I wanted this all over. I told him to back off, but he came back even stronger. I knew who the Old Bill would nick: it would be me! And I had to stop it. My pal, who's a rough diamond, threw the cunt off me twice. 'Fucking pack it in or I'll cut you,' I said. No response. He was fucking gone. So I gave him a little kick across the boat. It stopped him in his tracks long enough for us to get away from the mad cunt.

Fuck him! Anyone who does that to a woman holding a little baby deserves all they get. I looked at the bus stop to see if the woman was OK, but she had fucked off long ago, no thanks or anything!

A few days later at near enough the same spot, a man was stabbed to death after an argument with a group of young men. I rest my case: London is fucked up!

GIVING MYSELF UP

It was time to face reality, bite the bullet, face up, hand myself in, whatever you want to call it. For my sake and obviously that of my girl, and my daughter (who thankfully didn't know what was going on) and my nearest and dearest. Novelty had well and truly worn off!

My girl and I drove back to London so I could hand myself in. It was horrible. Two or three times, we nearly turned back. It was really emotional for us but I had to be strong for the both of us, even though I just wanted to disappear to be with her. I just wanted to be left alone! It was all fucking so unnecessary, but I had to face it.

We got closer to Bromley and my stomach was churning! I couldn't look my girl in the face.

We met Ola in a Lloyd's bar across the road. As usual in these situations, he was all business! I wanted a beer, anything to delay going in there, but he was having none of it.

I remember that, when me and my sort walked in there, some shy little cunt whistled at her. When I looked over, they all looked away – typical Bromley bastards. I wanted to run over and smash a glass in one of their boats. The mood I was in, I wouldn't have batted an eyelid. But of course I was in enough trouble already, and one look at my girl soon bought me round. I'd caused enough heartache for us both.

Bromley has a reputation for being a nice area but it's full of slimy cunts, black and white. Nice place, scummy people.

We strolled across the road, all three of us. For me it was like walking to the gallows. A bit dramatic to say that, I know, but I honestly felt dead inside.

I fucking hate Old Bill stations, I really do, especially the cells. For some reason they do my head in there: so claustrophobic, with no windows, just these shitty glass bricks about ten foot in the air. Why bother! They're just fucking concrete-and-steel boxes.

I know that may sound funny after all the prison time I've done, but I must say that I feel more comfortable in prison cells than police cells. If you ask a few bods that have done bird, they will tell you the same, of course. I would rather not be in *any* fucking cell, full stop.

We waited in reception and the copper who started all this shit finally came face to face with me for the first time. He was a short little jobsworth, as I had imagined he would be, as you soon realise a lot of the Old Bill are when you come face to face with them.

He went through his pantomime routine of saying hello, then reading me my rights and nicking me. I couldn't look at my girl, as we were both in pieces. I was led into the custody suite for questioning and charging. I said, 'No comment,' and was charged with aggravated assault on a publican. You'd have thought I'd given the Queen a dig!

Why publicans are held in such high regard is beyond me! They're usually ex-Old Bill (which explains a lot), villains or just muggy pissheads; a combination of all three is more like it!

After the hours went by, it was clear they were in no hurry to release me, so I told Ola to send my girl home. She was in such a state that she got lost on the way back to Pompey. I felt awful, but her coming with me meant so much.

Eventually, I was released on bail with strict conditions on where I stayed, and I wasn't allowed near the boozer (which I thought strange!). But at least I knew where I stood and, even though I had a court case hovering over me, I felt quite liberated. I didn't have to look over my shoulder, or jump out of my skin when I heard a motor pull up. Did I enjoy it? Would I do it again? What do *you* think?

CHAPTER 2
TRIALS AND TRIBULATIONS

Here I was again, on trial, at the mercy of the cunts, at the mercy of some fat fucker behind a bench!

Talking of the fat fuckers, when I first went up to plead, the prosecutor, who was only a young woman, for some reason took an instant dislike to me (the feeling was mutual). She tried so hard – bless her! – that at one stage I actually thought she might fucking burst! I kid you not.

My brief just kept calm. All *I* was up for was giving a barmy pub guvnor a slap (allegedly!).

I wouldn't mind, but I bet she goes easier on nonces than she did on me. But that's British justice for you!

Anyway, I was actually going to plead guilty, but, with the way the police brief was performing, I thought, Fuck it! I'll take it all the way. I used every trick in the book to prolong it.

It was Christmas 2007 and I didn't fancy being weighed off then, that's for sure. I wanted Christmas with my little girl, my fiancée and of course my family. Who doesn't? (After this one I'm not sure, though!) No one wants anything hanging over their head this time of year. It's all psychological of course: at the end of the day there's never a good time to go to jail. That's a fact. So, after a few approaches to plead, the trial was set for the New Year.

One of the worst things about going to court is having to mix with all the scumbags while you're waiting: you know, the cocky little rude boys who see going to court as a day out with their scummy pals or family. I remember when I was waiting to go in, and my girl said to me, 'Who's this mug looking at?'

Some little rude boy was fucking eyeing her up when my head was turned! Can you believe the cheeky cunt? I wanted to knock him out, but of course I would have been fucked. I walked right next to him and he wouldn't even look me in the eye. The fucking scumbag – he even had a sort with him! Well, I *say* a sort. She was a scraggy-looking thing who looked as if she'd been on the game all night and had then been dragged through a bush backwards for good measure. Proper vile. The typical sort of girl you see with these so-called rude boys.

I wouldn't mind, but he fucking stank and was pig ugly,

dressed in his finest tracksuit, which he'd probably had on for a week! Got some front, these ugly cunts, I tell you. I wanted to rip his head off! But it obviously wasn't the time or the place, and, anyway, he wasn't worth it. I remember his scraggly bird looking at me screwing him and looking at the floor in embarrassment that she was with the scum.

The moral of the story is this: if you take a lovely-looking sort to court with you, you could end up on a bigger charge. (By the way, Michelle was my rock throughout the trial, and I would like to particularly thank her for that.) And my advice is: if you *do* have to go to court with a little sort, make sure she's ugly! That way you won't get any grief.

So, after all the bollocks of the initial hearings, back and forth, it was heading for a full-blown trial in the New Year, as I said. I really wanted to avoid that at all costs, and was prepared to make a plea, if the cops would meet me halfway, as I had no faith in the system at all, and I had never got off a trial in my life!

But, earlier, the prosecution had smelled blood, and, because it was me, they stupidly took their eyes off the bigger picture and wouldn't give an inch. So fuck them! They left me with nothing else to do but take my chances at trial – and thank God they did!

The trial was set for March 2008. Did I have any faith in my chances? Honestly, no! I had been here before, too many times, and had left by the wrong door!

MY DAY IN COURT

And so came the day of the trial and my loyal missus had come down the night before from Pompey to be there with me. Things like that you don't forget. So the night before we tried to make the best of the evening – well, the best you can when you're facing the possibility of jail in the morning!

I'm a bad sleeper at the best of times, so I knew I had no chance of getting any kip at all, which ain't surprising. Michelle, on the other hand, is one of those people who can sleep on a clothesline, and how I envied her. I spent the night tossing and turning and being tormented by my own thoughts. So it was no surprise that, when the time came to get up, I was fucking shattered. But I didn't care: I felt numb, anyway. Nothing like a court trial, especially when you're the star of the show, to bring your senses up to date.

As we travelled to court, Michelle and I didn't say a word to each other. We just held hands and stared out of the taxi window into space. There was nothing to be said. The time for talking had stopped, and we both just wanted this thing to be over once and for all, this horrible cloud that was affecting our everyday lives. This is why I chose to go into the personal side of things a little more deeply in this book, and anyone who has been in this situation knows what I'm talking about – well, anyone with a life on the outside who ain't a scumbag!

Courts are lonely places to be, especially when you're up on your own. You find out who your friends are and, let me tell you, they are few and far between, out of sight and all that! Yeah, when that date comes when you have to face the music – and, believe me, it soon comes around – you do think to yourself, What the fuck have I done? How have I ended up here again?

But here I was and no amount of whining was going to change that.

My brief was Amanda, who was also a QC, so that wasn't a bad start. Although she came to me by accident, she might as well have been sent from the gods (and you will see why). I must thank big Billy for that. He's Spurs through and through and just happened to work at the same chambers as Amanda and, when by chance he was allocating the various briefs to their cases for the day, he came across my name on the list and diverted my original brief elsewhere and sent Amanda to me.

Amanda was an attractive, feisty blonde. But, believe me, she was all business. And it just goes to show how fate can intervene to give you a helping hand. And, let's face it, I needed a bit of luck, and it was about time I had some.

We went into one of the rooms, myself, my missus and Ola, to discuss the case. Amanda had gone to see the prosecutor to see if their witness was definitely turning up and if the prosecution might play ball. She came back and I could tell by her face it was a no-go. Once again the CPS

– the Crown Prosecution Service – were having none of it. Trevor Tanner on an assault charge and their star turn had pitched up.

My heart sank even more (if that was possible), but, as I said earlier, Amanda was all business and really tried her best to lift my spirits, bless her! I will never forget the look on her face as she stood watching me, helpless.

Ola seemed gutted to see me in this situation. You would've thought *he* was up in the dock instead of me. I've even tried to swap places with him sometimes, which is our little joke, but one I find hilarious, considering his dreads and boxer's nose. I've pointed him out many a time when they have called my name. I think it's hilarious, but he just looks at me as if to say, 'You fucking idiot!'

However, I could tell he was gutted this time. It was out of his control. He had done what he could and he was also my friend, which must be very uncomfortable for him! But I was now in Amanda's very capable hands. She had obviously heard of me and was well interested in the football side of things, which was quite funny, but made me like her even more. She had also represented some West Ham bods, who had done a good job of trying to annihilate one of our boozers. She'd got them off, too, which told me that she was up to the challenge straight away as far as my case was concerned. If she could get *those* cunts off, then I had to have a glimmer of hope. But, deep down, I really didn't hold out much hope.

So, there I was back in the courtroom sitting in a glass box with three senior magistrates to decide my fate. I took one look at them and honestly thought, I am fucked. I didn't even want to get eye contact with them. They were looking at me as if I were the scum of the earth, or so I thought! Now I more than anyone should know better than to judge someone, or a situation, on looks or appearances alone, but it is very easy to do.

The trial got going with both sides giving it all they'd got. It wasn't looking good. The pub landlord was up next and, when he made his entrance, my heart sank. He shuffled into the court wearing an old man's suit and glasses perched on the end of his nose, and he was blowing into an old hanky. Fuck this, I thought. I just shook my head in disbelief. And I noticed that the main bod on the bench, the chairman, saw this, too.

Amanda ripped the fool to pieces, though, and argued that, if he had been so badly hurt, why hadn't he gone to the hospital there and then? His answer was that he had to lock up the boozer. Also, she argued that there were three people involved, and, because I was the only person identified, how could they prove that I had inflicted the few bruises that he had? It was pathetic!

I've got no problems with the other two getting away with it. In fact, I was pleased for them, and in the end it probably did me a big favour. It would never cross my mind to give them up. But what really fucks me off is that there wasn't even a thank-you from them, or a drink sent my way by them or their people, which is bang out of order and something I won't forget. And I know who grassed me, don't I, Darren, you little cunt? Keep enjoying your drink, you grassing slag. You never know who might pop in for a drink with you one day (and, no, that ain't a personal threat, in case you're reading this, Old Bill).

I was convinced that my fame, notoriety, whatever you want to call it, in the football world was one of the major factors in my getting nicked. I mean, you only have to go into W H Smith to see my mug plastered over my book, or watch *The Real Football Factories*, a programme shown on Bravo TV, which was repeated endlessly with myself and Danny Dyer. Hardly gives you confidence for a fair trial, does it?

I was convinced it was a good enough argument to get it thrown out altogether, but apparently it wasn't, and this was a bit of a problem between me and Ola.

Before the trial started, I had denied everything. Which was my right. There were no CCTV cameras in the boozer, thank fuck. (It was installed the next day!)

I was invited to attend an ID parade before the trial. (Well, I say 'invited'. If you don't attend, you're fucked. If you do attend, you're fucked!) But if by some miracle you don't get ID'd, then you walk free – simple. I know, though, that they wouldn't have invited (that funny word again) me if they were not sure that I *would* be ID'd. Call me old-fashioned, but I'm cynical about things like that. And of course I did get ID'd and then charged. What a surprise!

Identity parades are fucking horrible, and it was the first one I had ever been on. They are not like you see in the films, though, when you see a motley crew of desperados lined up with an angelic-looking me thrown in for good measure, with a shifty little grass hiding behind a screen, with the Old Bill pointing in your direction (although it might as well have been like that in my case). It's all done by computer now.

You go into a room, sit down in front of a scary-looking tripod camera and then have your photo taken from different angles, all head shots, and they feed them into a computer. You also have to pick out, with your brief, so-called 'lookalikes'. Which is a fucking joke! If you have a shaven head, which I did at the time, then it would be geezers with shaven heads. If you had long hair, then the same goes. If I *looked* like something from a horrible little firm of inbreeds, then I would've held my hands up there and then, I swear!

PINKY AND PERKY GIVE EVIDENCE

But back to the court. Their star turn was now warming to his task and spluttering and stuttering away. He was looking like a fool. The prosecutor was frothing, which is a good sign. It was all surreal to me: it was as if I was there but wasn't there.

Next up were Pinky and Perky, as I like to call the two clowns that the Old Bill sent along at the last moment, and they were obviously briefed at the last moment, too – the original copper who had started all this bullshit in the first place had a massive heart attack. Before the case! He did survive, though, you'll all be pleased to know!

Pinky and Perky were being ripped apart by Amanda, much to the delight of my watching fiancée and my friend Simi, who were sitting just behind the clowns. One of them was a little short-arse who could just about see over the stand. And then he was calling the prosecutor 'your worship' and bowing his head every time he spoke, much to our delight. By this time, the prosecutor was telling him through gritted teeth to stop calling her 'your worship', as you obviously only address the bench as that, and even then not every two minutes!

Then she would ask him to look at his notes and on top of that Amanda was destroying him. This went on for a good 15 minutes. I could tell the bench were not impressed, and in the end the prosecutor just sat down. Next up was a tall copper.

He had a big moustache and looked like something out of the Village People. He had obviously gone to the same school of bullshitting as the other one. The scary thing was that he was actually there, and I was still getting evil looks from the bench, so I still wasn't hopeful in any way, shape or form. In fact, the old prison memories had come flooding back and I actually, mentally, started to prepare myself for being behind bars again.

If I had been single and free, then it would not have bothered me. But the fact was that I *wasn't* single and free, and that was the reason it would hurt more than anything. Sitting at the back of the court staring at me in my glass box was my stunning fiancée. It's every man's worst fear, the thought of having to leave his loved ones on the outside. And anybody who doesn't admit that is a fucking liar!

Don't get me wrong: she is as good as gold. We spoke about how we would cope with it if that scenario came about, and everything was cool. It's the snidey cunts on the outside you have to worry about more (you know who you are). Obviously, I would also miss my beautiful little girl like crazy. But I knew that she was still young enough to be shielded from the truth of the situation: you know, 'Daddy's working away for a bit', etc.

All in all, these things just add to the pressure of prison life. But, if it happens, it happens, I told myself, and there's fuck all you can do about it. If you're in there, you just have to get on and deal with it.

The trial was at the stage where Amanda was arguing that the amateurish photos the Old Bill had taken of the body weren't consistent – and, anyway, how could they actually prove it was me who'd done it? The prosecution looked well pissed off, and the bench seemed to be fuming at the whole thing. But, as they gave me only furtive glances, it was hard to see who they were pissed off with the most!

Suddenly, my counsel and the prosecution were in deep conversation among themselves; then the prosecution passed on the info to the bench, whose members looked at each other stunned. Fuck me! I thought to myself. I'm fucked. They're not even going to let me go the distance. Then, sure enough, it came.

'Stand up, Mr Tanner,' said the chairman. I got to my feet. 'We are going to adjourn for half an hour,' he announced.

What the fuck?

The clerk of the court then came up and opened my glass box, so I could stretch my legs, which I felt was decent of him. Now, you may think that was a bit stupid, but I had no intention of doing anything silly. After all, I wouldn't have handed myself in otherwise, would I?

I went straight over to my fiancée and gave her a hug. Likewise my friend Simi, who I hadn't known that long, but I won't forget how he turned up for me, as it gave me peace of mind to know Michelle had someone there with her. (He's a soldier in the Welsh Guards, and his morals are all in the right places. We'd had some good nights when he was based up the road from me in Victoria.)

We were all confused but everyone was trying to be positive for me, which was nice.

Amanda came over and told me the situation; and, to cut a long story short, she had called the prosecution's bluff and asserted, halfway through the trial (would you believe?), that there were serious holes in the case. What with the witness, and Pinky and Perky – and her being the clever girl that she was – she used a technicality that you can only use in magistrates' court, and demanded that the bench throw the whole fucking thing out.

Fuck me! I thought. If the trial continues, I'm royally fucked. And, because it's me and it concerns an accusation of violence, there's nothing stopping them sending me 'up the road', or 'upstairs', as we say. In other words, to the Crown Court, where I could easily be given some serious bird.

And so I was put back in my glass box and I waited, and waited.

And waited.

NO CASE TO ANSWER

The tension in the air was palpable, among both my people and the prosecution, who I think realised that, whatever happened, they had fucked up by not meeting me halfway at first. They could have got a lesser conviction, given me a slap on the wrist and everyone would have been a winner. But this was dragging on and, at the end of the day, was costing a needless amount of money, something that, in the current climate, I'm sure the bench did not take kindly to, even if they wouldn't admit it publicly.

I just sat there in my glass box not wanting to have eye contact with anyone. I went into a trancelike state, which I believe is a sort of mental self-defence mechanism.

Finally, the bench came out and the usher gave the all-too-familiar command: 'Please stand for the bench.' I stood, adopting my familiar court pose: upright, hands behind back, head slightly bowed, displaying a demeanour that said, Let's just get this over with.

'Sit down, Mr Tanner,' said the chairman.

This is not looking good, I thought. By now, I had resigned myself to the worst anyway. I was lost in my own thoughts, and at least I was satisfied that I had given it a good shot and my legal team had fought tooth and nail for me. At least that would be *some* consolation to take with me.

With these thoughts going through my head, I was oblivious to the heated exchange going on between Amanda and the prosecutor. I looked up and caught one of the bench looking, while the others were visibly shaking their heads. Fuck! I thought. I was numb inside by now. This seemed to be going on for an eternity, but in reality was over in a few minutes.

Finally, silence, and those words again: 'Stand up, Mr Tanner, please.'

The magistrates conferred with each other one more

time and there was a general nodding of heads in obvious agreement of something.

The chairman of the magistrates spoke to me for about two or three minutes, telling me in as much detail as possible what had happened and was going to happen. I swear I cannot recall any of it apart from these few words: 'No case to answer. Please release the prisoner. You are free to go, Mr Tanner.'

I looked over to my left to see my fiancée and my pal punching the air. Then Amanda came running towards me, still all business until she got right up to the dock. And then she broke into a big smile. 'Come on, mate. We've done it. You're free.'

I couldn't believe it; I stood there in shock for a moment. This couldn't be happening to me, could it? Things like this just *don't* happen to me. But, as the dock door was unlocked and I was reunited with my loved ones, I started hopping around the court like a demented kangaroo.

Well, I had just won a court case. That's my excuse and I'm sticking to it! If the bench had seen my performance they would have locked me up for sure. But I couldn't give a fuck what I looked like. Suddenly, the world was a good place to be, and the adrenalin rush was amazing. I still get a tingle to this day, as it had never happened to me before.

I obviously gave my fiancée a great big hug and loads of kisses first, then whispered a thank-you in her ear. Then, once we were outside, everyone got some loving: Amanda who I would like to say a big thank-you to; Billy, for putting her on to me; and, last but not least, Ola, because, without him, none of this would have been possible.

Then I became aware that one of the coppers was heading towards me. I bowled up, threw my arms around him and said, 'How do you feel? Cheers, mate, you were brilliant!'

He looked stunned and so did I when I realised what I was doing. My missus came over and guided me away. I must have looked like an excited puppy.

Give him his due, though: he took it well and was actually smiling away as if to say, Fuck it – it's fuck all to do with me anyway.

But his pal was looking gutted and a lot less pleased. Time to exit stage right, I thought.

We all decamped to the boozer across the road – the White Hart – as is tradition. The drinks were on me, and they *really* started to flow. Everyone had a silly grin on their face. I was high on adrenalin, absolutely buzzing, so the booze was having little effect on me. It was great to see people so happy for me. Amanda loved asking me about football, which was brilliant coming from a QC (well, it seemed like that at the time), but in my book she had earned every drink and more, that's for sure.

Billy had by now joined our little party and he seemed more happy for me than I was, which was terrific. I know a geezer called Jacko, who had a lovely little boozer right opposite, and we decamped there. Amid all this kerfuffle, I had to go and sign on at the police station and hand my passport in, as Spurs were playing in Europe.

Once back in Jacko's bar, I felt that it was a lot more relaxing. I had met him on a personal level only a few weeks before, and, like all the top boys, he was always polite. When he saw me with my girl and entourage, he came over to join the party, bought a drink and was well pleased for me as any proper man would be. He's got a lovely place in Bromley, which is a club at weekends, which he says I must try.

By now Simi was pulling Amanda's hair like a five-year-old, and Amanda – bless her! – was well tired. It had been a fantastic evening but it was time for taxis all round. It was also time for me to be alone with the other half and let the real enormity of what had happened sink in. Better than drugs – trust me.

CHAPTER 3
GOING BACK

It was a long time since I was allowed back over to Spurs – a lot of water under the bridge and all that. Sunday, 20 January 2008, to be precise, was the day I chose – Spurs versus Portsmouth. Well, it *had* to be, didn't it? Although I am banned from the ground itself for life, my actual banning order was finally up, allowing me once again to go into the *area*, and see some old friends.

I'd had to wait a long time for this and, I must admit, I had mixed feelings and was even a bit apprehensive. But I needn't have worried, since I got a great reception from all the boys – apart from a bit of a drama in the snooker hall later in the evening. It was somewhere I didn't want to go in the first place, but, having been bought my umpteenth Jack Daniel's and Coke by my generous pals, let's say I wasn't thinking very clearly. The little incident was fuck all to do with me, but no doubt I'd get the blame, I thought. All I remember is some tall prick standing in front of me asking if I was going to cut him. The fucking fool! If I wanted to or had a reason to, I would have. But I was just sitting down having a chat, minding my own business. A pal had kicked it off with them somehow while they were playing snooker. Mind you, he could start a row in a phone box, let alone a snooker hall, but nevertheless there was no need for it.

I nearly bit at the end, but luckily my good pal Kieran was there and he managed to get me out of the door before I could risk having *another* charge slapped on me. I was annoyed with myself, though. I should have gone home a lot earlier. It always gets messy when you don't. Too much drink and, before you know it, there's too much of everything flying around.

But, all in all, it had been a good day, and I'd stayed later than I should have. However, I hadn't seen some of the people I was with for years, so I was naïve to think it would be a quick one. (And I'm probably being a bit hard on myself!)

THE TROUBLE WITH SPURS

On the pitch Spurs were fucking shit, whatever their manager, Harry Redknapp, said. Not being able to finish off a crappy Pompey side at home? It's an absolute disgrace. And with that complete waste of space Darren Bent missing an open goal in the last minute! He must have thought his days were numbered. I had the right fucking hump with that prick, as that game meant a lot to me (or missing it did!). The trouble is, before Harry came to Spurs, they'd bought a load of so-called stars who, since coming to the club, have turned into different people overnight.

(As we were to see, in August 2009, Bent eventually signed for Sunderland.)

During the final days of the Juande Ramos era before Harry Redknapp took over, they were bottom of the League and all that. But Harry turned up and the rest is history – and we went on an unprecedented run of seven wins out of eight matches.

The trouble is, the season had been turned on its head. All the teams at the top, like Chelsea, the Gooners, Man U and Liverpool, and even fucking Villa, kept on winning. The teams everyone thought would roll over for an easy three points – Hull, Stoke, Bolton, etc. – continued winning as well, which threw a real spanner in the works for us, and I'm not blaming Redknapp for this either. I reckon that, considering the clowns he had at his disposal, with anyone else at the helm we would have been fucked. But the fact is that, even with Redknapp clearly busting a gut to improve things, we were still bottom of the table. I know that with a few wins you can go halfway up the table, and I'm sure – well, as sure as I can be – that we will be fine and still a Premiership outfit when this book comes out. But, let's face it, as I write this, our defence is fucking useless. And who knows how costly that open-goal miss could be at the end of the season?

Redknapp was right to have a pop at him publicly. Fuck him! He's on 40-plus grand a week at a time when people are losing their jobs everywhere. If someone in a factory fucks up an important job or order or suchlike, something that they would normally do with their eyes closed, then in these financial times the poor bastard would probably be out of a job.

Let's just hope we don't reach another final and get relegated. It shouldn't happen, but it's a possibility. Harry needs to get his own men in, and fast. And as for Ledley King. He's either got to call it a day, or have it done for him. Sounds harsh, but everyone knows it's the truth.

THURSDAY, 22 JANUARY 2009

What can I say? I had my little girl last night, so I couldn't even get to watch the game, and it should have been a foregone conclusion. But this is Spurs. I got a text about 9.30pm:

ARE YOU WATCHING THIS SHIT WE'RE 3–0 DOWN

I couldn't believe it. But, in reality, I wasn't surprised. We are shit at the moment. I couldn't help but take a sneaky look on Sky Sports to see the result, and of course it was true.

I was getting a few texts through that only someone who knew me well had the bottle to send. But you couldn't blame them, really, as we were on the brink of one of the biggest Cup defeats of all time, losing 4–1 going into the second leg as 100–1 odds-on favourites to go through. To give Burnley their credit, they were two minutes from putting us out, but they didn't: we scored three late goals to shut all the wankers up once and for all.

I suppose that, if you're on 60 grand a week, the least to be expected of you is you can run fast!

Anyway, we're through to another final, which is not to be moaned at. And in the League Cup, too. Man U in the League Cup!

It was great to see the boys again, people I'd known half my life, people who have stood side by side with me on many occasions, whether we had a result or not. The drinks were flowing and I felt like a returning king. It was so difficult not to get carried away by the whole atmosphere. I'd wanted to come back out of the cold, back into the warm embrace of my firm, my people. But the old saying is true: nothing is ever the same again.

However, the old feelings came flooding back. The adrenalin was flowing and I was itching to get out on the street and mix it up a bit. But I knew I couldn't: I had made promises that I would keep my nose clean.

LOSERS

It's Saturday. Manchester United versus Spurs, 24 January – and, as expected, Spurs have gone out to the Mancs. Deep down, as soon as the draw was made, I knew it would happen. It was on the cards. Now everyone knows the old cliché: there's no shame losing to Manchester United at Old Trafford and all that bollocks. And there's no doubt that some teams look beaten before they even start.

Losing against that lot I can just about handle, but not even *trying* is unforgivable. I don't give a fuck what position we are in the League – that's their own fault. But, like a prick, I'd put a score on them to win. I'd been giving my missus earache on a drive back into London to find a bookie's pronto. We ended up in my local one in south London (you don't find many on the motorway!). The game had started and we were 1–0 up. My bookie was only too happy with my score. (They must have been laughing their bollocks off as I walked out the door.) With a big grin, I bounced back to the motor.

Roman Pavlyuchenko put us in front with a blinding header. After that, though, it was a different story. To cut a long story short, they were a fucking disgrace. We were strolling out of the biggest cup competition in the world. Never mind the 6,000 fans up there (and my score!). Redknapp threw his toys out of the pram and went ballistic. The sad thing is the Mancs aren't that great and were there for the taking. It could have been great but it wasn't.

And who scored? Those slags Dimitar Berbatov and Michael Carrick, that's who – both a couple of greedy cunts. But it's our fault for selling them to Man U and taking the money. Instead, we should've told them both to go and fuck themselves, and that they'd have to stay for a couple of years. And we should have told Man U's manager, that horrible red-faced cunt Alex Ferguson, to stick his money where the sun don't shine. We have got a Premiership-chasing team. Simple.

KEEPING A LOW PROFILE

The Old Bill hadn't realised that I'd crept back on the scene, which was good, as I could keep a low profile for the Pompey game. I even got a black cab from Victoria to throw them off the scent a bit. But it won't take long for them to realise, and then it all begins.

The landscape over Spurs had changed quite a bit since I was last over there with the usual musical chairs of visiting different boozers. What the Old Bill don't realise is that they can shut down as many boozers as they want but, at the end of the day, whether they like it or not, there is one of the biggest football clubs in the country stuck slap bang in the middle of Tottenham. And the boys are going to drink somewhere – regardless.

When they shut boozers, they just pass the grief on to some other poor bugger. I know a lot of landlords who've given up and moved on because they couldn't take the shit the Old Bill were giving them because of us. One of them, Seamus, was a very good friend of mine, and his family had owned the Corner Pin for years. What people don't realise is that these people really rely on match days for their living, because, during the week or when there aren't any matches, the boozers are just full of assorted nutters, and the area itself is a total shithole. Put it this way, you wouldn't want to be strolling around there at night without knowing people.

At the moment, the place of choice is the Billy Nick (the Bill Nicholson, to give it its full name) and, when you compare it with the rest of the boozers, it isn't hard to see why. The fella who runs it is a nice geezer and has made a real effort getting DJs Brandon Block and Alex P playing there on big occasions. Oh, and having loads of sorts behind the bar obviously doesn't do any harm.

As you can imagine, on match days it's chocker, considering that the last boozer we drank in was a Wetherspoon's house, which was fucking horrible, so there isn't much competition. There are loads of little boozers dotted around, tucked behind the high road, such as the Vic and the Beehive. All are handy for ambushing any unsuspecting little firm who fancy their chances. It's really just a constant battle between the landlords, the Old Bill and us.

The Old Bill have even given out booklets of photos of so-called 'known faces', telling the landlords not to serve us and to call the cops instead. It's not enforceable – just the Old Bill getting themselves at it. It's outrageous and a breach of civil liberties. When the guvnor of one boozer – which I won't name, obviously – showed me my mugshot, I was fucking fuming.

They must have photographed me on a bad day. It's bad enough that they have a picture of your boat behind the pump, but when it's a bastard one it's out of order (I may sue!).

As I said, things have changed a lot over the years. What were the youngsters, or yoof, are not kids any more, and some of them are bigger than I am. I'll go into more detail about yoof in another chapter, but everyone around the country, especially West Ham, knows how game they are.

The landscape has changed and, as it's done so, they have evolved. Mind you, West Ham are getting a bit naughty and keep turning up with all their old monsters, because their so-called yoof lot just aren't up to the job.

There are a few new faces on the scene, which is natural – some good, some bad. And, unfortunately, there are still a few cunts around who you would have hoped had fucked off altogether. One such particular little scumbag came up to me at the Pompey game.

He's a busy little shit, and I wanted to rip his head off, since I'm sure he's a grass. The worst part of it is that he comes across from south London. Every firm has them, unfortunately, but, on the whole, they are a great bunch of boys.

Banning orders have been dished out like Smarties at a kids' party – some, admittedly, to those who deserve them. But some are just pathetic, like some that were handed out for shouting a bit of abuse at Sol Campbell; and a 15-year-old was dragged through the courts in Portsmouth for shouting at a football match, along with 11 others of various ages, up to their forties. I know one of them. These people could lose their jobs over this. The reason Campbell is hated at Spurs, and always will be, is that he let his contract with us run down, then forced a move (he left Spurs in 2001 and went to Arsenal before moving to Portsmouth in 2006).

Fuck him! Fair enough. We've seen a lot better than him move on, and will do in the future, no doubt. But, rather than go to Milan or the Mancs, he wanted to stay in London. The rest is history, and the cunt went up the road to the scum Arsenal. He kicked us all in the teeth by doing that and will be hated down the Lane for ever.

I actually feel sorry for Pompey, who are in the shit with that idiot Tony Adams in charge. And they're having to shell out 60 grand a week they cannot afford on that useless lump of shit Campbell. Watch him jump ship at the first opportunity. *That* is why we hate him – end of.

I feel better for that!

A TRAGIC DEATH

As I said, the landscape has changed big time because of banning orders. I'm convinced the Old Bill have got some sort of rotation policy whereby they won't have any given number of faces over there and active at one time. While I was over here, a lot of the boys were there having fun. And, when I was allowed back, half of them were nowhere to be seen. Coincidence? I don't think so. It was good to be back, though, and, as I wrote this section, we had some big games coming up: Gooners, and Man U in the Carling Cup final at Wembley (which would turn out to be a 0–0 draw, but with Man U winning 4–1 on penalties).

I admit the banning orders have hit our firm hard, there's no doubt about that. Also, a very good friend of mine, and my ex-partner in crime, Martin, is now doing a two-and-a-half-year stretch in one of Her Majesty's prisons, along with another good pal, John. It was a naughty scene, which I won't go into detail about. They were attacked by a little firm in a horrible estate in southeast London, while having a benefit night for Martin's disabled daughter. Unfortunately, they picked on the wrong firm and it ended with one of the attackers dying at the scene, which is tragic. But it was not directly anyone's fault, so they were on attempted-murder charges, which were reduced to violent disorder.

I'm sure they will agree with me that two and a half years is not a bad result, even though they didn't deserve anything at all. The fella who died was spraying CS gas around a boozer with a very ill child inside it, which eventually cost him his life. It was all over the London news and it was portrayed in the media as a gang-related football row between Spurs and Charlton fans. But the boozer was bang in the middle of the estate where Martin and his family live and they were entitled to be in there, especially as it was a benefit night for his little one. Obviously, the local little firm took offence to the boys being there, and it ultimately cost a man his life. So, out of respect to the dead and the fella's family, I will leave it there.

And in another tragic twist, Martin's wife died suddenly of a brain haemorrhage at 39 years of age, leaving behind three children, who Martin is now bringing up on his own. The dignified way that he handled the funeral and his trial has given me more respect for the man than I can say. His missus and I used to have some right old dingdongs over the years, but it was all good-natured, so, wherever you are now, rest in peace.

A SOLDIER IS LOST

Terry Salmons, another old soldier, is doing time as I write, after a naughty row at King's Cross with Oldham. I think a doorman took a hiding in the mêlée, which is what he got the bird for. No doubt Tottenham Old Bill would have stuck their oar in. My brief Ola looked after him. He pleaded guilty and got three years, which he is happy with, as it looked at one point as if he might get a ten stretch.

So we've lost a proper soldier for some time to come, because, if the Old Bill get the slightest whiff of a football-related incident, he'll probably be given a nice hefty ban as a going-away and coming-out present (just like me). The Old Bill are thoughtful like that.

His brother, Steve, was also a friend of mine. He was shot dead years ago, and I know that Terry had the hump because I didn't mention him in my first book, *Tottenham Massive*, but I didn't want to say things that were very personal. However, Terry told me Steve would want to be remembered, so I will say just one thing: Steve, my very old friend, wherever you are, God bless, brother.

Some bods over there always seem to be there and never get nicked. Which is a bit suspicious if you ask me. It seems that there are too many people who have all the glory and talk a good show but don't want to take it that one stage further – the point of no return if you like. The Old Bill are getting on top of things, as people don't want to risk it all with the silly sentences they hand out for football violence (take my three years for instance).

It's 2 February as I write this, and we're languishing at the bottom of the table with the Gooners at home on Sunday. Shall I go? What do you think? And it wouldn't surprise me if we beat them at home.

I know you may laugh, but it's the same old Spurs, different manager, different players, apart from Jermain Defoe, who just won't go away (he was with Spurs from 2004 to 2008, and is now back again after a spell at Portsmouth). Bottling it away from home, as usual, our players are fine in front of 36,000 of our own, but when it's at someone else's house they don't like it, that's for sure. I think they think winning home games will be enough. The dangerous thing is that they are running out of them, and – surprise, surprise! – Robbie 'I've always been a Red' Keane wanted to come home because Liverpool didn't fucking want him (he did come back eventually – more on that later).

SNOW OVER LONDON

It's February 2009 and, as I'm writing this, England, and especially London (which is really weird), has woken up to a snowstorm. I kid you not. I'm sitting here in my local library (you thought I was going to say boozer) and it's been snowing all night and day. They reckon it's the worst snowfall in 18 years in London. I can't remember it ever

Top: Top: Me in the middle, looking a Teletubby. Did too many weights back then – looks like I ate them! But this photo was too good to leave out. Next to me is the late Tony Lambrianou, on the right is Tricky, Gregory Foreman (Freddie's son) and my old friend Greg, then guv'nor of The Punch Bowl, the pub later bought by Guy Ritchie.

Middle: The boys at Epsom races, waiting on a visit from West Ham (who didn't show!).

Bottom: Eighty-handed in Southsea, Pompey – brilliant day.

Top left: Me and Blocko! Brandon Block is a top DJ and a good friend.

Top right: Stevie D, looking well scary after being nicked for the Parsons Green bloodbath.

Bottom left: Me and Griff.

Bottom right: Me and George (Irish). We go back years.

Above: Me and Nobby, 92. And a chance for me to respect the memory of all the friends of mine who have served and those who lost their lives in Afghanistan.

Middle: Steve and Craig – good friends and top boys. And a big help with this book.

Bottom: Me and the boys just after we scored against the Scousers.

Top left: Me and Luds.

Top right: In my local in South London with Campbell (Rob). He's a good fella and friend (game as they come).

Bottom: I took my little girl to see the Trooping of the Colour.

Top left: Me and Brandon striking another pose! Superstar DJ.

Top right: Kevin Phillips plays for Birmingham FC. He is a mad Spurs fan – very polite, very nice fella. We had a few beers and a laugh!

Bottom left: H and Sandy the dog in the summer of 2009 in Tottenham.

Bottom right: Kali is Spurs yoof, a great kid and a great help to me with this book. Thanks mate!

Top left: The guv'nor of the Bill Nick. It's a great boozer in the back streets of Tottenham.

Top right: On Blackfriars Bridge.

Bottom: Big Andy is an ex-marine and a friend from Pompey.

Top: The back yard of the Bill Nick. Liverpool at home! Some very old friends in this picture.

Bottom left: The horse belongs to my girlfriend's uncle Mark. You don't get many of those in South London. This was taken in Pompey.

Bottom right: Kenny is yet another one of my old friends.

Top: Me and Craig again. Good photo. End of.

Middle: Celebrating as Spurs score.

Bottom: Me by the pool of our apartment in Portugal '09. Waiting for the taxi to take us home. Great memories!

being like this before. I'm thinking of calling for a couple of Huskies and a sled. It's great to look at but, as usual, everything has come to a complete standstill. No buses or trains – as if the lazy fuckers needed an excuse. So it starts to become a pain in the arse.

It's been predicted that it's going to kick off big time tomorrow night in London, and, for some fucked-up reason, the fixture list has put several clubs all in London, all using the same Tube network. Happy days. You couldn't make up the stupidity.

The Old Bill will be swarming all over the Underground with dogs – sniffer dogs especially. Their best little toy. The fucking things – I hate them. Not that I have anything to hide, of course. I just think that it's wrong to use them on football bods. It's a breach of civil liberties, let's be honest.

The majority of bods pay ridiculously large amounts of money to see the matches, and they can't afford to watch a bunch of overpaid cunts in the freezing cold. A lot of them are weekend warriors, who save up and look forward to their Saturdays with the boys – as I did, once upon a time. Now you have the Old Bill with sniffer dogs at stations, and, even worse, I was told that the snidey cunts had them inside the actual turnstiles when we played Pompey at home – hidden out of view until they pounced on you like a fucking trick-or-treating clown. Pathetic! What for? Nicking family men. I was told that ordinary Joes and little boys were being carted off. So what if a geezer wants a little bit of sniff or suchlike to keep him going during his day out? It's a fucking joke. It's just more tactics by the plods to prise people away from football altogether.

Silly cunts don't realise, though: no football means no easy nickings, and no overtime for doing fuck all. It's as if anyone would be silly enough to have anything incriminating on them. It's just fucking up people's lives for the sake of it, while down the road people are getting shot and stabbed. Good to see the Old Bill have their priorities right.

Don't get me wrong: I'm all for those dogs that sniff for explosives to stop those terrorist slags, although those cunts either blow themselves up or are too clever to be caught. But nicking football bods, who are mostly good people, for having a bit of personal is a fucking liberty and I despise them for those tactics. It's bad enough living in the fucking shithole without having sniffer dogs up your arse at every corner.

That's told them!

It's just another thing to add to the banning orders. I was starting to ask myself, Do I really want this shit? Do I want to carry on until the experience gets too negative? Do I want to throw a cloud over all the great times that I have had in the past?

Anyway, it's still snowing and I'm halfway home.

Dodging all the little bastards with their snowballs. (Don't they know who I am? Ha, ha.) They have probably got rocks in them. So I have done what every Londoner does when it snows: go to the boozer. And it seems like every other fucker has had the same idea.

And for a few days at least, London had been transformed from one of the most miserable cities to a winter wonderland. Shame it doesn't snow at Christmas, when it's *supposed* to! Still, there are still quite a few games left as I write this, and I intend to get stuck into at least a few of them.

This Carling Cup – the League Cup – is an obvious bonus and I was really looking forward to it, as I'm normally on a ban when they come around. And obviously, with the Mancs in the final, I reckoned it should be lively off the field, too – hopefully, bit of fun, no one too badly hurt, and no nickings. Perfect day out (if only!).

I'm going to leave a little chapter free for that one.

As I mentioned earlier about the game we had with Burnley in the semis, fair play to them, they came to London early. I think they landed at 10.30 or something silly like that. And full marks for the effort they made to come down undetected, as well.

So it was all set. Except that they didn't read the script. They disappeared into central London for the day, which is fair enough. But the thing is, if they had gone straight over to Spurs, they would have had a result. As usual, we were not taking the so-called smaller teams seriously, which is silly, but there you go.

They reappeared later on in the afternoon and called it on. When the boys moved there, Burnley moved to Finsbury Park and got the Old Bill all over them like a rash. Game over.

RETURNING

As this chapter is about my going back, it seems that old Harry Redknapp is keen on making me eat my words, or trying to make a bit of a mug out of me. The old sod! He's not only brought Jermain Defoe back, but he's brought Keane back, too – then fucking Pascal Chimbonda, after his spell at Sunderland. Is he having a pop at me or what? I stand by what I said, though, about them all. Keane has made a fucking fortune out of transfers (and so has Defoe). There's no doubt Keane fucked up big time by going to the Scousers. I just knew it would end in tears up there for him.

Personally, I think Harry should have splashed out on new blood in the shape of the Russian Andrei Arshavin, who ended up going to the scum Arsenal, which is a worry. But Keane is back now, and even though I might not like some of the players, or the way they go about things, I bleed blue and white, and, if we have a hungry striker with a point to prove (let's face it, he couldn't go to anyone else), and he scores bags of goals to keep us up, then happy days. Time will tell. Oh, and Spurs made a cool £8 million on him. So that may have something to do with it.

The firm has lost a lot of good boys down to banning orders, prison, death and the Old Bill just making a fucking nuisance of themselves. But our yoof firm are very strong and active, and, backed up by the rest of the boys, were a formidable force in our day, that's for sure. More importantly, Spurs are a very streetwise firm that will always survive. It's good to be back.

CHAPTER 4
THE SEQUEL

Since I decided to write this book, my head has been so full of shit that that it's been blank, if that makes sense. I'm sitting on Southsea beach in Portsmouth. As you know from the first book, *Tottenham Massive*, it's one of my old haunts.

I've got a lot of mixed emotions about the place now, as I have got my fiancée down here, as well as family. It puts a whole new perspective on things. Put it this way, there are a lot of scumbags down here who could do with a slap. But I also have a few very good pals there as well.

Second day down here, and my mind is still a fucking blank. Yesterday was 90 degrees Fahrenheit; today it's blowing a fucking gale. The final straw is getting my bottle of beer blown clean off the table. Bollocks to it! I'm going inside. That's out of order.

Me and my missus are looking after a place owned by a good pal of mine for a few weeks. Just off the seafront. And because I normally have to fork out fucking fortunes on hotels, etc., as I'm back and forth every week to see my girl, it's a welcome relief for my wallet. He is a great little fella, one of life's real characters. He has also got a set of decks, and 5,000 records to play with, which makes it an even nicer stay. So, Paul, I promised you a mention and there it is, pal.

It's been a really hectic few months. It's also been a really hectic couple of *years* since the last book and all that went with that.

I've got no regrets whatsoever about doing that last book, even with all the shit I took (behind my back). It's just fucking jealousy, and all you cunts know who you are. Contrary to what people think, I never made a fortune from it. (Why do you think I'm doing another one? Joke!) Every penny I got was spoken for, or spunked up the wall.

I must admit that, when the book first came out, it did go to my head a bit. And anyone who has been in a similar situation and hasn't done the same is either a boring cunt or just a liar, or both.

What I didn't realise, like a prick, is that you get your wonga only every six months. It's just something you have to deal with, but it's a total head fuck.

THE STREETS OF LONDON

Going back to what's happening in London at the moment with all these horrible little cunts stabbing each other, why don't they just make it illegal for people to walk around in hoods during the day or night – especially night? They have obviously got something to hide, haven't they? Horrible little shits. The thing that makes me laugh is the silly little pricks wearing hoods in the middle of the summer (smelly bastards).

Terrorising old ladies and men my mum's age must make you very proud, you pricks.

Personally, I couldn't care less if they carried on wiping each other out, until there is none of the little scum left.

I've been sitting with my beautiful little girl, Elle, on the top deck of a Routemaster – the last one left in operation in London. It was fantastic, took me right back to my childhood.

It's a shame that cunt Ken Livingstone, London's former mayor, and a Labour government have had so long to destroy the city that I once adored (notice I said 'once').

When I started writing this book there was always some sort of drama going on. At the moment everyone seems to have the hump with me. Especially my missus, who, if I didn't love her to bits, I could quite easily strangle (tried that and it don't work!). We have been together for a year and a half now and for me this always seems to be a dodgy period. I'm sure it will make us stronger (I really

59

hope so). Things wouldn't be half as bad if people would just mind their own fucking business and stop interfering.

Since I came back from Portugal, after crashing a bike and getting a third-degree burn on my leg, I've now fallen off a ladder trying to cut my hedges (don't laugh). Then, after a row with my missus, I've booted a brick wall (how sensible) and fucked my foot up completely.

So I'm now sitting in King's College Hospital surrounded by foreigners, pissheads and silly fat birds falling over – with every one of the cunts being seen first. Just been seen by the triage nurse and it looks as if I have really fucked it up. Next, I'm sitting in A&E being prodded and poked around waiting for an X-ray. What a way to spend a bank holiday! My X-ray is causing a right scene. Happy days!

What am I going to do? Always getting something. At this rate I will be writing this book from a hospital bed.

I'm now in the fracture clinic and I have been booked into an appointment for 9am in the morning in the new block. I thought things had changed, but I should've known better. Seems like half of fucking London has the same appointment. It's full of foreigners and weirdos. I'm sure half of these cunts spend their nights here.

New place, but the same bullshit. Hundreds of people with the same appointment. Don't get me wrong: I'm not complaining about the staff, the majority of whom are as good as gold. Some are well fucking moody, though. Dealing with scum all day must piss them off big time.

MILLWALL V. SPURS – PRE-SEASON GHOST GAME

It's the end of July 2008. Saturday the 26th to be precise. Which also happens to be my little one's birthday. I've been getting calls all week from one of Millwall's boys, foaming at the mouth at the prospect of playing us again.

I couldn't believe it at first. Surely, after the mayhem of the last time we played them, the Old Bill just wouldn't let it happen again. Would they? Alarm bells were ringing. This has got to be a setup, surely. We caused turmoil over there last time (just a few summers back). We really took it to them, with the best firm seen over there in many a year. If the Old Bill hadn't rounded us up and surrounded us ten deep at Surrey Quays, I dread to think what would've happened.

My Millwall pal was well excited about it. As I had crashed the bike in Portugal, had a third-degree burn on my leg, which had to be dressed every day, and had a fractured foot, I was obviously out of the game. But, if it was happening, then I would certainly get the boys up for it.

I made some calls and got a strange response. Nobody knew anything about the game. I must admit, I wasn't too happy with the response. I was hoping a 'been there, done that' attitude wasn't settling in because that would be bollocks. Then I made more enquiries and drew more blanks. This was fucking strange. What was going on? I had Millwall in one ear adamant that it was going ahead and my lot in the other ear adamant it wasn't. Proper head fuck. I checked all the usual things, in the papers, fixtures lists, etc., and came up with fuck all.

Someone was either pulling my plonker or this was a ghost teams' game. As you have probably guessed by now, it was played behind closed doors and not advertised at all.

Behind closed doors or not, I still can't believe that the Old Bill let it go ahead. Of all the teams that we could have played! They might as well have made it Chelsea and be done with it. Don't get me wrong: I would be well up for it. It just didn't make any sense.

I have to be honest and say Millwall were well up for it and my lot were on their holidays. Harsh, but true. In fairness to us, everyone had their eye on the tournament out in Holland with Feyenoord (can you believe?), Celtic and some muggy Kraut team. By the time everyone realised it was actually being played, it was too late, but, as I said, I wasn't happy with the response.

I walked into a boozer on the river, which will remain anonymous and spotted all their young firm on the first floor straight away.

Me, Elle and H sat outside on the river, as we were taking El for a meal. As I said, it was her birthday. They had obviously been on it all day and some of them were well smashed, which ain't a good combination. I got a few looks but nothing major and I'm glad to say they observed the rules that you don't go for someone with kids or their missus in tow. You always get some slag who might try to break that rule, though.

So we moved to another gaff around the corner. Well, fuck me! There were several of their older bods plotted up. How's your luck! I was only going for a Pizza fucking Express. Thankfully – and I wouldn't expect anything less – the same rules applied. There were a few startled looks when they clocked me. I was hoping they didn't think this was our firm, just me, Elle and H!

CHAPTER 5
(NOT SO) HAPPY BIRTHDAY!

Birthday time again. Chelsea on the Sunday two games into the season, and two losses on the spin – to two mighty teams who go by the names of Middlesbrough and Sunderland. I really would like to say that I am surprised. But I can't. It's a typical Spurs start to the season. When are they going to learn to stop the hype and keep their fucking mouths shut?

I know it is early days still, and I am optimistic that, with the quality we have brought in, we will come good. The fans deserve a good season for following them everywhere – even when they are shit. But fair's fair, and it's only just started, so let's see what rollercoaster we are on for this season.

First of all, though, I had another fixture that comes

around once a year, my birthday. It's been a weird year in lots of ways, don't you think? Everything has come early. I mean, bank holidays seem even earlier! Normally, my birthday falls on or near the August Bank Holiday weekend, the weekend of Notting Hill Carnival. If you can call it a carnival. Gang rapes, stabbings, shootings, 350 arrests. And that's not including the 200 or so little cunts they stopped going. Personally, I would ban the fucking thing. Some carnival!

I think a time is coming, though, when people will have had enough of it – black and white. And, until these horrible little lowlifes learn some respect and how to behave, maybe pulling the carnival might get my city back to normal. Or they should get involved in football firms and learn a bit of respect.

As I said, my birthday was looming again. I must admit that, although I was really looking forward to it, spending some quality time with my friends and what have you, I do have my reservations. Let me fill you in. Have you ever had a birthday party from hell? Well, that is what last year's one turned out like. People getting knocked out, glassed, you name it. I'm not kidding. Looking back, I realise it was my own fault in a lot of ways. I was too casual with the guest list and just let word of mouth do its thing. Trust me, that's a bad mistake. Don't get me wrong, they were all my own people there. And that, I know, makes it sound even worse. We had Birmingham at home that afternoon, so you can see where this is leading, can't you?

Basically, I turned up sober with my missus ready to party. Also, my missus had family there: her sister and a pal had come down – although that caused a right load of grief. All I was trying to do was look after her. The moral of the story is not to fucking bother.

I should know better, of course. I've seen it before. You try to help someone out (watch their back) and, because all the time they can't see that, they turn on you, and, if it's a bird, stab you in the back. Anyway, the boys had turned up in force, but that's all it was: just geezers. And they had all been on the sauce all afternoon at the football.

Basically, it was like a fucking queers' convention. As you can imagine, I wasn't happy. I was on edge all night. But every other fucker enjoyed themselves, don't worry about that. That is what fucked me off more than anything: that some of these cunts had the front to turn up at my party in that state in the first place. And, as far as I'm concerned, anyone who brings someone with them who plays up is just as responsible.

And obviously, with my missus there, I couldn't relax. Any decent man would be the same – it's natural, ain't it? Don't get me wrong: none of my close people would dare to do anything untoward (or so I thought) but you have to be on your toes, as experience tells me that you always get one pissed-up cunt who can fuck it up in minutes. I felt sorry for my pal who had come all the way down from Birmingham to London, bringing his wife down with him, to be surrounded by a load of pissheads.

It makes me laugh with a lot of geezers and, it has to be said, the football bods. You invite them out, bring your birds as well, and they turn up on their jacks or with ten geezers. What the fuck is that all about? What part of 'bring your bird' do you not understand? It fucking makes me laugh. I'm sure a lot of them are scared of birds, or, closer to the truth, they don't mind being around other geezers' birds, yet they haven't got the confidence to bring one of their own. Harsh words, but fucking true, and they know it. And I'm not just taking about my own people here: it's across the board. But I'm not worried about other people – only my own or people around me (if that makes sense).

I'm sure any girls out there will be nodding their heads with me.

As I said, a lot of the boys were lagging but behaving all the same. One of them was acting like a cunt and I fucked him and his pal off. I wasn't going to let all this shit spoil my night, though, so me and my missus just got on one. Everything was cool, but I knew deep down that it wasn't to last – and I was proved right.

Little did I know that this incident would start off a chain of events that would lose the friendship of pals I had known for 20 years. OK, it wasn't a perfect night, far from it. And it wasn't what I wanted, but there you go. My pal James was deejaying for me, which he did at the last minute because I was let down by another prick who I won't name (Andy) who was meant to DJ but pulled out the night before (class!). I should've known how the night would go.

Four or five of my pals were from Palace and, as I've said, we go back years. They are just local pals at the end of the day. One of them in particular (and you know who you are) was well pissed. Mind you, he was no more pissed than I or anyone else was, really, and he *always* sounds smashed. I think years ago he copped a hiding or had an accident, which isn't his fault. But make no mistakes: he is one of the top boys and as game as they come.

I could see him having a bit of banter with one of my close pals and it all looked good-natured, although I know from experience he can be a right fucking nuisance. He is one of these bods who, especially when they've had a drink, try to climb all over you when you are speaking to them. Which is one thing I personally can't stand. People who invade your personal space – there's no need for it.

What I didn't realise is that the bit of banter had turned the other way. What I hadn't clocked was that Mr F (I'll call him that to spare him any embarrassment) had been jabbing my other mate in the face with his fingers and generally making a nuisance of himself. But I hadn't seen any of this. All I saw was a good friend (*was*) walking straight into a right-hander and getting knocked spark out, with a couple of snidey cunts giving him a few kicks for good measure (that I still ain't happy about, as it was fuck all to do with them).

But then a sense of being in the wrong came over me. How *dare* they do that at my birthday do, in front of my family? A groundswell of rage came up from the pit of my stomach and I screamed at my pal, 'What the fuck do you think you are doing?' My fist was clenched and everything went into slow motion. I think everyone was waiting for me to throw a right-hander, but I wasn't going to stoop that low.

'Get the fuck out of here!' I screamed. 'And take all the cunts with you.' And so off they skulked.

The Palace bod literally didn't know what had hit him and I felt really sorry for him (like a mug). I somehow felt responsible, which is bollocks, as it had fuck all to do with me. But that's just the way I am (unfortunately): carrying the weight of the world on my shoulders.

We picked him up and dusted him down, and, thankfully, apart from a few bruises, he was OK. I tried to make sense of it all and swore to him that, when I caught up with the boys, there would be murders for it. He seemed happy with that (well, as happy as you can be when you have just had a proper clump) and, after a brief interval to wipe away the blood, the DJ, like all good DJs, carried on playing and we all tried to get back to normal, having a dance, a drink and enjoying ourselves.

One thing I did find a bit strange was that the bods who had brought him along didn't seem that concerned. Alarm bells should have been ringing. Towards the end of the night, everyone filtered off home but I had the flavour now. And, after dealing with drunken pricks and all the other shit all night, I just fancied getting home with my missus, her sister and her mate and relaxing for once, which anyone is entitled to do in their own home, aren't they? Surely nothing else could go wrong, could it?

Yes, you guessed it. Honestly, you couldn't fucking make it up. So we called for a sherbet and, soon enough, one came.

PUTTING THE RECORD STRAIGHT

Now, so much has been said about this incident, mostly lies, by people who weren't fucking there and seriously just want to stir up shit and listen to only one person's side of the story. I have really wrestled with my conscience on this one, as it is a private matter. But, because all of the crap being bandied about, I think it's only fair that I get my chance to tell the truth. I couldn't give a fuck if they want to go on believing the shit that this mug has spouted. I know the truth, and so does he. And this is it. Here goes.

Four of us shared a taxi. Me, my girl, her sister and her friend, who was staying with us that night. But standing outside the club on his own was the same bod who had got a clump. Once again, he was left by his pals, which was strange, don't you think? Again, alarm bells should have been ringing. I jumped out of the cab to see if he was OK. He said he had no money, and couldn't get home, although later my missus told me he had pulled out a big wad of money. So what was the cunt up to?

Anyway, I didn't see that and I felt sorry for him standing there like a little boy lost, especially as he had got a hiding at my party. So I did the honourable thing, which I think most people would, and took him home in our cab (what a mug!). He doesn't live that far from me and I thought that, as I already had guests staying on, he was up for a little after-party drinking. I thought it wouldn't hurt to invite him home for a couple. To be honest, it was just to make me feel a little better after my pal had clumped him. Deep down, I knew he was a nuisance and I shouldn't have had him anywhere near me or the girls. And, as soon as we got into the cab, my instincts were proved right. Something changed in him. From being the victim, he suddenly became all cocky and lairy. And it soon crossed my mind that I had made a major fuckup.

My girl's sister and her pal were acting like a couple of kids and having a wind-up with him, as birds do when they are together and pissed. Ordinarily, it wouldn't be a problem, as it was a happy occasion, but I could see that, in his state, the silly cunt probably thought he was in with a chance.

I was in the front of a people carrier with him; my girl's sister's mate was behind me; and my missus and her sister were in the back. I told my missus's sister to pack it in, then I lost it and screamed at my missus to shut up. I felt bad that she had copped it from me like that, but it was really directed at him, and it wasn't my place to bollock her sister and her mate, even though they deserved it.

Anyway, we got back to my place, stuck some tunes on and cracked open a bottle of Jack Daniel's and tried to salvage what had been a fucking shit night. I thought everything was OK, that we were all just a bit nutted and just acting like kids. But I could feel that something wasn't quite right. This mug kept getting too close to my missus for comfort. He kept touching her arm and getting in her space. I told him to behave a couple of times. So he can't say he wasn't warned. I went upstairs for a piss and when I came down I could see he was up to his tricks and had put himself right next to my bird, who was by now near enough in the wall trying to get away from the pest. Then I saw his arm slide down and get too close for comfort again. He knew he had done a wrong 'un and tried to make out it was an accident.

'Fuck off, you piss-taking cunt!' I spat at him. 'Get the fuck out of my house!'

He then squared up to me, the cheeky cunt. I punched him open-handed in the throat, and down he went again for the second time that night, like a sack of shit. (Wasn't his night, was it?) My bird's sister and her mate looked on in shocked silence. Fucking great! This was *all* I needed.

'Come on, fuck off, you mug.'

I grabbed him and marched him towards the door. We were in the hallway and approaching the front door and I was prepared to leave it at that, as I had known him for years and we had all had a drink, although at the time I felt stone-cold sober. It was just him and me now on our own, with the only barrier being the front door. And I swear this is the truth and not the bullshit he has been spouting to anyone who gives a fuck.

As I went to open the door and fuck him off, a right hand suddenly slammed into the side of my neck. I couldn't fucking believe it. The cheeky cunt! I instinctively slammed a right-hander into his face. The only problem was, I had a glass in my hand and a bit of his ear came off, which I found the next morning.

But I never meant to cut him, and that is the fucking truth. It was just instinct and I didn't realise I still had a glass in my hand. And, if he hadn't acted the cunt and then swung at me, it wouldn't have happened. But, at the end of the day, he got what he deserved and, in all honesty, trying to pull stunts like that in my own house, he is lucky I didn't kill him.

The repercussions of all that went on for months with every cunt having his say. I was made out to be some sort of fucking monster, when all I had done was look after the girls. To be honest, that actually hurt me more than the row with the prick, and it annoyed me as much, too, if not more. It's bollocks having your character assassinated by a bunch of jealous cunts from afar. Especially when you can do fuck all about it.

Me and my girl, though, were as strong as ever. Thank God it has all died down (until this account comes out, anyway). I just felt the truth had to be told. And I found out afterwards that the mug was making silly faces behind my back in my own home (what a cunt!) and my missus didn't want to say anything (bless her!) because she didn't want any trouble. Disrespectful prick! After I had taken him home, paid the sherbet and given him drinks, too.

I later found out that he had instigated the grief at the party as well by jabbing his finger into my pal's face. As I said, it wasn't his night. But all joking aside, it really did fuck my birthday up. And I took no satisfaction from giving a geezer I had known for years a clump. But, at the end of the day he left me with no choice. He should learn to keep his hands to himself – then there is no excuse. I would expect the same if it was the other way round – not that I would do anything like that. He got what he deserved, simple. The sad thing is, I copped it from both sides and haven't spoken to some bods I have known for the best part of 20 years. Let the mugs believe what they want. This is the truth and deep down they know it.

CHAPTER 6
SUMMER LOVIN' '08

Still on a ban. No football. No Euro '08. We didn't qualify, that's why. Oh, yeah, we are in some Mickey Mouse tournament in Holland. What did I tell you about that ginger tosser of an England manager, Steve McLaren, and his team of jokers? Well, he got the push for it, didn't he? And his assistant, Terry Venables, went with him.

I can't believe David Beckham, Rio Ferdinand, John Terry, Frank Lampard, etc., and even Jermain Defoe. Still coming out with the same old shit. Golden generation, my bollocks! Beckham's finished. Not that he really ever gets started, and all the rest ain't that far from the end. And, with our national side's track record, and big tournaments coming only every two to four years, I would say we are fucked.

I know a lot of people have fallen out of love with the England team, the players in particular. It's ironic that, as I'm writing this and having a pop at the cunts, they have just gone and beaten Croatia 4–1 in a World Cup qualifier in Zagreb, ending a 35-game unbeaten run (see, they fuck me at every turn). With that little Gooner slag Theo Walcott scoring a hat-trick. Credit where credit's due, though: that was a good result. It ended a 15-year unbeaten run at home for Croatia, and I don't care what people say: Zagreb is a hostile place to go. It just goes to show what the lazy shits can do when they want to.

And let's not get too carried away, because Croatia aren't as good as England have made them out to be. That's a fact. Go back five, ten years ago and you wouldn't have given them a chance. It was easy street all the way with Beckham, and co. He even picked the fucking ponce when he had a broken foot. You couldn't make it up.

It must have been a head fuck for other players, who were playing out of their skins and rightly thinking, I'll get a call up here, as it should be on form alone. But not under these two clowns. They rolled out the same old cronies, Becks (as he likes to be called by his close friends), the two Chelsea cunts Terry and Lampard, Ferdinand, Steven Gerrard and that dog Wayne Rooney. Even if they were having a shit season, they could all rely on the old-pals act. Well, that's so fucking sad!

MASSIVE ATTACK

The only good thing to come out of not qualifying for Euro '08 was that it left Sven's idiotic sidekick McLaren with nowhere else to go. But trust me, I would rather we had qualified and then got rid of the pricks. What the FA and the players don't seem to grasp is that it's not all about them, it's not a jolly boys' outing for the mugs, and it's not about how much dough the WAGs can spend on moody clobber and fake tans. No, it's not for the players. They are overpaid. They should just play for their country and keep their mouths shut and their birds locked up somewhere safe. Like Holloway! No, they just don't realise what a big international tournament means to the *people of this country*. I know they bang on that they do, but if you believe that then you're a mug. Half of them live in a fantasy world, with 50, 60, 70 or hundred grand a week. Come on, deep down you really think they give a fuck whether we qualify or not? I don't think so.

To most of them, England is just a publicity machine. That's the real reason the little fuckers turn up. Especially you know who. (I won't mention his name because you will all think I'm paranoid.)

You see, they need England whether they like it or not. Because being an England international keeps them in the public eye and keeps their parasite agents happy because they rake in massive endorsements, sponsorships and image rights – and it keeps the players happy with loads of supermarkets to open.

All they needed to do was put in a half-average performance, get another cap and get another supermarket. Everyone's a winner. And they wonder why they're all getting drummed at home, etc. when they let their birds get photographed with ten grand's worth of shopping on them. And they're showing off 50-large watches, when half the bods who pay their wages are on the dole. Something ain't right, is it? Something's got to give, surely. Someone has to stop these thick cunts getting paid so much dough.

The way this country is going, I wouldn't be surprised if in the future we have players being kidnapped and held to ransom, as is common practice in Mexico and South American countries such as Brazil. I would pay good money if someone would kidnap the whole Chelsea team. That would be fucking brilliant! Anyway, sorry about that.

So, as I write this bit, we have a whole summer of discontent to look forward to.

SUMMER OF DISCONTENT – OUT OF EURO '08

Yes, that's right, out of Euro 2008. Knocked out by that superpower of world football, Croatia. I won't go on about the games. We were just shit, simple as that. We lost away to Croatia and you all know what happened at Wembley, when they bottled it with the infamous 'wally with the brolly', Steve McLaren, slowly sinking into the Wembley turf.

Brand-new stadium, too, which we didn't need. Why did they have to knock down the towers? That was just fucking sacrilegious. There really was no need for it. But it's no surprise really, as that is what we are good at: ripping down a hundred years of history and heritage. And, of course, the left-wing councils won't object.

So we had the laughable fact that the country that invented that game wasn't going to be in Austria and Switzerland. All I can say to the team is, 'Thank you, you useless bunch of cunts!' I was well up for going out there and mixing it up. I've only had to wait years for the privilege and it's not too much to ask for, is it?

But, then again, I should know better. This is England we are talking about, the great underachievers, the team that always bottles it when it really matters. Harsh, but true. So, while the Poles, Germans, Dutch, Turks and so on had Austria and Switzerland to themselves for a month, all we could do was watch from afar like gatecrashers who haven't been invited to the party. And all the above cunts would be strutting around giving it large in the safe knowledge that England fans wouldn't be there.

And the thing that made me laugh was the coverage it got over there with Gary Lineker and his pals. Talk about rubbing salt into the wounds! But most of the scummy other European countries at the Euros would be happy, especially in London, because they are all here anyway.

So I had to watch the likes of 'pretty boy' Rooney getting married slap bang in the middle of the championships. What a cunt that is! As I said, they don't give a shit. Don't get me wrong: he has every right to get married to that funny little bird. Just use your common fucking sense and spare a thought that the whole country has the fucking hump.

It's fair to say that the England team ruined a lot of people's summers. I know that sounds dramatic but it's true. Your ordinary man in the street can't afford to fuck off to the Seychelles with a poncing little tart in tow for a month until the whole thing blows over. I think the FA and their clubs should put a banning order on the useless cunts (like the one *I* was on) to stop them travelling abroad or going on the piss in public, etc. while the tournament is on, as punishment for being shit and not qualifying. Not too much to ask, is it? I'll tell you something: if something like that was in place, then we would qualify for fucking everything, *whoever* was in charge (expect McLaren). Fantasy talk, I know.

I mean, we are on to a loser for starters when you have the Premiership, i.e. Fergie, Arsène Wenger and Benítez, telling the FA when and when *not* to play games, and more or less picking the England team by not releasing certain players. In any other country, they would be told to fuck off and run out of town. Not here, though, not in good old Blighty. I mean, come on, do you honestly think that Fergie (a Jock), Wenger (French) or Benítez (a Spaniard) honestly give a fuck about the English team? Of course they don't.

So let's return to the summer of 2008. Not only didn't our muggy footballers step up to the plate, but the weather didn't bother to turn up, either. As it turned out, it was one of the wettest summers on record, and we were approaching the end of September. It was all over bar the shouting. It was a bit like having 12 months of winter. Because, thanks to the England team and the weather, most people never had a fucking summer. Fuck knows how much money the economy lost with England out. I mean, pubs, clubs, shops, supermarkets, stalls, you name it – they would all have been packed at least a few times a week for the best part of a month (or at least for two weeks before we got knocked out at the first proper game; sorry, but it's true). I mean, you would have had half of England out there watching it, swamping the two countries. The stadiums, bars, hotels, etc. That alone would be worth a fortune, surely. I don't care what anyone says, it was quite sad seeing the England flags at half-mast draped outside windows.

It was a bit like the hosts of the party forgetting to turn up. You had the TV channels with Gary Lineker and his Scottish mate Alan Hansen chucking it down our throats every two minutes – advertising a tournament that no one wants to fucking know about. Boozers were desperately trying to entice people in to watch Austria versus Romania (as if!). I for one, and I'm sure a lot of the boys would agree with me, couldn't give a fuck about a tournament if England are not playing.

You always get a few sad cunts who will watch two flies going up a wall, but I'm sure most people would agree Euro 2008 never fucking existed for us, thanks to two useless cunts – you know who you are. I couldn't give a fuck if England were to go on to be undefeated in all their World Cup qualifiers and go on to lift the fucking thing in South Africa in 2010, and I hope they do. And with this Italian, Fabio Capello, in charge of the national side we may have a chance, as he looks as if he won't take any shit from these pampered mugs. The jury is still out, of course, and it's very early days, but the signs look good.

I touched earlier on how they are obviously shit scared when they play at Wembley in that fucking 90,000-seater monstrosity. But, what with the public opinion of these people at an all-time low, I really believe that they all fucking knew that if they got beaten again in Croatia there really would be nowhere to hide for them. I'm convinced they used the fear of failure and being slaughtered left, right and centre, and thought, Fuck this – we are miles better than these cunts (you only have to look at the two we signed – not Modrić). There is no way we are coming home this time without a result. We just don't need the fucking grief.

Of course, the rest is history. They played a blinder and put the Croats firmly in their fucking place, where they should have been two years back. That's the annoying thing – on their day, England can beat anyone. On and off the pitch.

With a weak manager, it's about whether or not they can be bothered. Maybe with a stronger one in Capello, who won't let the fuckers slack, who knows? They really could come good this time around.

Hope springs eternal and all that. And don't get me wrong: I love England with a passion. I just don't like the players. And, whatever they go on to achieve, and I hope it's to lift the World Cup (in my lifetime). The fact of the matter is that they should be ashamed for ever for letting the whole country down and not qualifying for the 2008 Euros, while superpowers like Romania, Ukraine and the fucking Czech Republic were strutting their stuff. And we weren't invited. Not a lot to ask.

CHAPTER 7

2008, PORTUGAL – A FEW YEARS TOO LATE

I missed the last Euros in Portugal, when we were actually fucking there. So my missus and I decided to get away for a week, to escape the doom and gloom over there. No footie, shit weather, nasty little cunts stabbing other nasty little cunts (with a few exceptions) on an almost daily basis in London.

It was all getting out of hand, or – correction – it *was* out of hand. Fuck knows why London house prices are so expensive, as, at the moment, it's swamped with foreigners and is a shithole. Portugal was having a heatwave and it was up in the 90s Fahrenheit every day. I thought I would have some of that. The only thing I wasn't looking forward to was the flight. To be honest, I just don't like it (oh, and it scares the shit out of me). I mean, what is enjoyable about sitting in a space not even fit for a midget, with a lottery about what prick you are going to get next to you? Or behind you, or in front of you? And don't get me started about the airport.

This was to be my first holiday in ten years, as, let's just say, the Old Bill fucked my holiday plans up with their over-the-top antics. As you all know, I had just come off a five-year banning order, whereby my passport was effectively doing a five-year bang-up. It got so bad at one stage that I didn't know if I was coming or going, what with the games coming up thick and fast and changing the Old Bill stations I had to report to, that in the end I just used to leave the poor fucking thing there.

But back to our holiday. We grabbed one of those last-minute deals off the Internet. Don't ask me how. I don't have a clue. I just left all that shit to my missus (except paying for it). Anyway, we were all set, no going back now. The funny thing about holidays is that they always seem to come about at the wrong fucking time. I know what you are thinking: there is never a bad time to have money, and that's true to an extent. What I mean is that, if you're anything like me, fucking shit with money, it'll be in one hand and out the other. I always seem to have a bit of wedge when I don't really need it, if that makes any sense. Let me explain.

It's January, February, March and you've got a few quid wrapped around you. Summer's coming up so I think I'll stay in and do some fucking knitting. Or go out and spunk it on a month-long boozer? Yep, you guessed it, I would stay in and do some knitting (like fuck!). Maybe if I did I would have a few quid. Obviously, it doesn't help having a long-distance relationship, spunking money on hotels, meals, nights out and what have you. But anyone in the same boat as me will understand what I mean: when you and your loved one don't see each other all week, you live for the weekends.

Then you go totally mental, chucking money about as if it was fucking confetti (which you can't afford), basically overcompensating because you have been apart for so long. Then during the week when you are on your jacks looking at four fucking walls, talking to yourself, you go out on the piss (naturally), spending even more money you can't afford, nine times out of ten surrounded by some dickheads you normally wouldn't give the time of day to. And when birthdays (and the fuckers always come up firm-handed, don't they?), holidays, Christmas and so on all come up you're skint. Bollocks, ain't it?

I was well nervous about flying, and getting myself wound up on the way to the airport. I was scraping together a bit of cash for spending money, right up until the moment we got on the plane, which was a load of bollocks and stressed me out even more, as I'm sure you can understand. The sherbet that took us to the airport had a shitty little motor, driven by an African who I had rows with in the past. Happy days!

But we were going on our holidays, so I really tried to hold it down, as we both needed the break: me, well just because I'm me and all that it brings, good and bad; and my missus because she works hard all year in a shitty factory and her mum had only just got the all-clear (thank God) after a battle with stomach cancer, which resulted in her having her stomach removed – literally. But she is still here and getting stronger every day, bless her, thanks to the brilliant treatment she receives at Queen Alex Hospital, Portsmouth. So big shout to them! Also to the old girl. We fight like cat and dog but I love her to bits. Hope she knows that (well, she does now).

The sad thing is that my own mum has to put up with the lottery of the NHS in London. I'm not blaming the doctors or nurses, who, by and large, are good. It's those people who call a fucking ambulance if they stub their big toe.

Anyway, you get the picture – we needed a break. My missus said to me on the way to the airport, 'Why don't you stop at the cashpoint on the way and get your money out?'

'Nah, it'll be sweet,' I said. 'I'll get it out over there.' Anyway, what a fuckup that would turn out to be.

We arrived at Gatwick and I paid the African his dough. 'Forty-two quid return?' I say. 'Yeah, bruv, cheers.'

Then he says, 'No, man,' and tells me it's £42 one way and to return it's £48.

'What you on about, you silly cunt?' I say, ready to explode.

Anyway, to cut a long a story short, it turned out he was right. It *was* £42 one way. The prick in the office had got it wrong.

I was well pleased with myself all week thinking I had a right result. In my defence, it has been ten fucking years since I was let out of the country. What can I say? The fares have gone up a bit. People did try to tell me, but I was having none of it.

CHAPTER 8

SPURS IN CRISIS? WHAT CRISIS?

Well, before I start, I'm going to have to hold my hands up and admit to getting things wrong and eat a bit of humble pie. To cut a long story short, we were eight games into the new season and Spurs, then under the staring, despairing eyes of Juande Ramos and his gang of fools, Damien Comolli, Gustavo Poyet and some fitness guru guided Spurs to our worst start in over a hundred years. Or, in case you have been on another planet from the start of the 2008 season, since before WWI.

We had lost to Stoke away in the League, which is pathetic. No disrespect to Stoke, but we are Tottenham and they are, well, Stoke. On top of that we played like clowns against Udinese and lost 2–0 in the first group-stage match of the UEFA Cup. Now I was one of Ramos's biggest defenders, especially after we beat Chelsea in the Carling Cup – something that none of us will ever forget.

When you look back on it, those sad staring eyes were totally vacant for weeks, that wild-eyed expression. He looked the part with his Desperate Dan chin. You shouldn't go by appearances, but he seemed to be shedding the tears of a clown (just about literally in his case). He was like a rabbit caught in oncoming headlights and all that bollocks. Fuck knows what happened to the once great man of Seville, the man with the greatest UEFA Cup pedigree on the planet. Don't get me wrong, I don't feel sorry for him: he was paid a fortune – and then some.

I remember sitting with my missus when he gave an interview. If you can call it that. My missus asked me who this mug was and I pretended I didn't know. Then up came a caption with his name.

Now I think that being paid the best part of £4 million a year entitles your employers and supporters to at least understand what the fuck you are saying. He obviously thought having that Chelsea cunt Poyet as his translator would be enough. Wrong. In between his stuttering lingo, my missus and I were watching what was to prove to be one of his very last interviews (thankfully). Among his stuttered words came an almost minute-long whining 'Eeeeeh, eeeeeh', as if his batteries had fallen out. We both looked at each other and burst out laughing. I'm telling you now, I would learn fucking Chinese quick time if I had been offered a £4 million contract. And the club's chairman, Daniel Levy, got it spot on sacking those two clowns with him. Good riddance to bad rubbish.

I know in the past I have slaughtered Levy, and there is no doubt he has made some fucked-up decisions in his time at Spurs. And he has got to take a large portion of the blame for all the messed-up wasted years he has presided over. But in that one night (and here is the humble pie I'm eating) he went from zero to hero in one giant leap.

It was a fateful night in October 2008. All Spurs fans had gone to bed with the hump, with the prospect of being humiliated by shitty Bolton the next day. I had actually had a nice night and been up the West End for a few bevvies with my girl and we were quite happily merry when we got in and I crashed out. But I'm a crap sleeper so I decided to watch the insomniacs' favourite, Sky Sports News, in bed for a while. And that fucking scrolling caption thing that glides by at the bottom of the screen – you need ten goes to make out what it says. 'Ramos sacked,' I caught. 'Fucking good job!' I shouted, nearly giving my girl a heart attack.

Then I read, 'Redknapp is the new Spurs manager.'

My jaw dropped and I just slumped back into the pillow in complete stunned silence before waking the dead with a scream of '*Yes!*' I didn't believe it. It had to be a wind-up. Was I fucking tripping or having a bad dream? I woke up in the morning and discovered that, yes, sure enough, it was true: Harry Redknapp had come to Spurs. It wasn't a dream.

Now I haven't exactly been complimentary about Redknapp since he moved to Tottenham Hotspur, and, to be honest, I'm not sure why. But deep down you have to admire how he gets teams going from afar. He's obviously his own man and any fool can see that there's lot of character hidden beneath the hound-dog looks – although, if I remember rightly, he had his boat smashed up back in 1990 in a car crash during the World Cup in Italy, which obviously is not his fault. This was the one in which Bournemouth's managing director, Brian Tiler, was killed, along with four other people.

Now I'm not going to get carried away and make any rash predictions. And, as I write this, we are still rooted to the bottom of the table and, yes, we could still go down, although it would be a travesty for such a massive club. We have taken one point from three games and I couldn't give a fuck whether they were last-minute goals, own goals, whatever. We have been done like that by both the scum teams, Chelsea and the Gooners, for years.

We have had some right clowns down the years as managers, too, no doubt about it. There was Christian Gross, for instance, with his Travelcard (hope he never got a weekly). What a tosser he was! Then David Pleat, boring Gerry Francis, traitor Glenn Hoddle (went to those scum, Chelsea). All of them, and more, had one thing in common with Ramos. They were all shit.

The players obviously wanted to play for Harry. You only had to look at Bent, who was on fire (as we've seen, he moved on to Sunderland in July 2009). And we had now taken nearly maximum points from our last few games with a 1–2 win over Man City, which was an excellent victory and a sign of a new era, as the Spurs of old would have dropped points, that's for sure. The bottom line is that Harry had put the players in their preferred positions and the results are there for all to see. I'll hold my hands up and admit (a bit more humble pie here) I got the man completely wrong. I never thought he would leave the cosy little setup he had at Pompey; I don't think anybody did.

It's been well documented about his big house in Poole and he is obviously not short of a bob or two. And, on top of that, he had turned down a few other big jobs – although you can't blame him for turning down all that bollocks up at Newcastle.

But it seemed that he was obviously driven by something far deeper than money. And obviously this was a chance to prove himself at a massive club, and a London club to boot. London's where he comes from, where he was born in 1947, a place where he trained in the 1960s in his West Ham days, when he was a starry-eyed kid.

This was too great an opportunity for him to miss. And, with the start he made, Spurs can thank their lucky stars.

The only thing that can fuck it up is us, Spurs themselves. As long as the chairman Levy sticks to his word and lets him manage the way he likes, then I can see only good things for us. But, if Levy and his cronies interfere, or start to move the goalposts (as it were) even slightly, then I have no doubt Harry would walk away. Let's be honest, the man isn't shy about doing that, is he? I hope for his sake, and ours, that he doesn't. After all, he's redeemed himself in the eyes of all the fans in one go. Harry has been itching to get his teeth into a truly great club, a massive club like ours, for a long time and I couldn't give a fuck what anyone says: there ain't a bigger club, not on history alone, let's face it.

The Mancs have massive support, of course, but most of them live in China and Guildford. Fucking joke, really. As for Chelsea, I read that they're after building a new 75,000-seater in Battersea. What's the point of that? The silly cunts can't fill up the shithole they have got now, so where are they going to find an extra 30,000 people? I suppose owner Roman Abramovich can always buy them!

I hope they do move to a new ground, as it will have the same atmosphere as a morgue. Of course, old Roman is no fool, and the real reason he wants to move house is that Chelsea's ground sits on probably one of the most expensive pieces of real estate in the world, and he knows that, by moving the fools to a piece of wasteland by Battersea Power Station, he will get all his wonga back, and them some. And hopefully fuck off back to wherever the ugly prick came from.

But this is about Harry, who, whatever happens in the future, presided over a miraculous run of results to lift us off the table.

Obviously, I know how pissed off they are in Pompey with all this. No one wanted to lose a man like that, and the way some of the silly cunts down there have behaved you would think I was personally responsible for his coming to Spurs. But the fact of the matter is, he turned Spurs down a few years ago out of loyalty to Pompey, so he owes them fuck all. He left them in the top half of the table with a squad they could only dream of, the majority of whom, whether they admit it or not, went there because he was there. Not only had he left them flying in a league they really don't have a right to be in, but he has also left them in Europe for the first time in their history.

Oh, and they could have kept that lairy little cunt Defoe: we didn't need him. I couldn't give a fuck what anyone says, he is well overrated. Let him stay on Easy Street, I thought while he was down there, because he can't hack it at a proper club. Knowing my luck, I predicted, by the time this book comes out, Harry will probably have brought him back again. And he did.

So, apart from that, Harry has fucked up some of my earlier predictions. I thought it was going to be one crisis after another. Instead, it looks like he has stopped the rot. And the only way is up – as long as Levy leaves him alone. And the same goes for those busy cunts at the City of London Old Bill. Give it a rest, eh? Crisis over. What crisis?

CHAPTER 9

BRANDON BLOCK

Brandon Block doesn't need any introduction from me, that's for sure. From young ravers to boys and girls in their forties and fifties – yeah, and upwards – most of you have probably heard this popular club DJ's music at some stage in your lives, unless you have been shut up in a silent order.

He and his friend and fellow DJ Alex P are both mad Spurs fans, and played a blinding set for the boys over at the Lane, which I know was well appreciated. Brandon's one of your own and hasn't changed from the day I met him, even taking my phone calls when I've been off my nut. And I've been asking him to listen to me destroy a tune while I'm telling him how good I am. Sad, eh? But that's friendship.

When I went to interview him for this, I got stung for £20 by the hectors at Watford Station. I thought Watford was in London Travelcard territory (how thick is that!). Well, every other moody little town is. Only joking. We had a top afternoon, even ended up losing my brand-new phone. Couldn't work the fucking thing anyway. So, all in all, the afternoon cost me a fucking fortune. But it was worth it, and he's a good mate even though we don't see each other often because we're both all over the place.

I think this might make people think about me in a different light: I'm much more than football violence, always have been, and a lot of other football bods are, too. The music scene has always been an integral part of my life, and I'm sure that a lot of boys and hopefully a lot of girls will find this interesting, and enjoyable, and maybe think I'm not just a one-trick pony. This is our chat, enjoy (oh, by the way, TT = me; BB = Brandon).

TT: All right, broth. Good to see ya again.
BB: And you, broth.
TT: How long you supported the Spurs?
BB: All my life. I was brought up at Spurs. My old man used to take me and my pals straight from primary school to the Chante Clair – the Hotspur club.
TT: Fucking hell, broth! I remember that, with the Spurs carpets and all the players bowling about. They never used to let me in there.

BB: Don't forget I was a kid. I met Steve Perryman, John Pratt, Glenn Hoddle, and Jennings when he was there, Martin Peters; that was lovely in there, you can imagine, for a young boy of seven or eight. It was great fun.

TT: Yeah, I bet it was, you namedropper! I would be like it now, although if I had been there the beginning of this season, 2008/2009, when we were rock bottom those players would have got a dig no doubt. The players you're on about, though, are on another level. Legends. End of.

BB: Yeah, my dad—

TT: Yeah, Harvey, lovely man.

BB: Yeah, he was in the clothing industry. He used to work for a Jewish firm, and they was in with the Spurs management at the time. And they made all the suits for the FA Cup against Man City.

TT: Yeah, I remember it well. A wonder goal by Ricky Villa.

BB: Yeah, that's right.

TT: Yeah, I was on a ban – for a change.

BB: So I met Villa and Ardiles, when [Keith] Burkinshaw was manager, so it was good fun, great days. It's just a fucking great club, Tottenham, ain't it?

TT: Yeah, it's in the blood. How long you been a DJ for, broth?

BB: For 24 years now.

TT: Do you still enjoy it as much as back then?

BB: Yeah, I think so. You get your moments. I mean, it's more of a job now. When I first started it was just fun in the pub with your mates. We used to get paid 30 quid between the three of us, and that tenner used to get us up to Umbreys in the West End on a Friday night. Do you remember that gaff?

TT: Fuck me, of course I do. Well scummy gaff, full of sluts and Arabs. You must have seen me in there.

BB: That's right 50p a drink. You remember.

TT: Not fucking much of it.

BB: Fucking 50p, broth, 25p on a Tuesday. So we would have our tenners each, then go round the boozer and ask everyone for a pound each.

TT: You weren't stripping, was ya, broth? That's a Flying Scotsman King's Cross trick.

BB: Yeah, go on. So we would head up West with our dough. You stick a pony behind the ramp and you could get fucking rat-arsed all night. How much we used to drink!

TT: Don't bear thinking about, does it? When did it really start to take off for you, broth?

BB: About '87, '88. Me and my pal started deejaying together. You probably know him. He was a Gooner, one of Denton and Millers boys.

TT: No comment.

BB: Anyway, he's one of my oldest pals. Anyway, it was

one of them pub chains when they first started doing the pubs up, putting music in, flashing lights and all that. And the group at the time said, as we put on such a good night, could we do some more of their boozers? So we bought some mobile equipment, bought a little yellow Commer van, an old BT one, and we'd go round London doing our thing in various boozers. Then you just meet people. And then we progressed on to the club scene. Eighty-eight, I started a great big club in Ealing called Broadway Boulevard, that had a banging night on a Thursday, called Zigzags Club, so I did a few events for them lads. So you just meet people, and that was it.

TT: Snowballed from there, then, broth?

BB: Yeah, we had Ibiza '91, then I ran my own club in Ealing for a while, and there was Queens, Full Circle, Sherman, all the sort of clubs we used to go to, and it started from there really, mate. I suppose, late eighties, early nineties, it started going well and I had to give up working. I was working for me dad in a printing factory; I was warehouse manager, believe it or not.

TT: Nothing wrong with that, broth, it's a job.

BB: Yeah, I know, but it's not what I wanted to do. So I was out every night of the week, DJ out of me cake. I never used to go home. I used to go straight to work and sleep in the warehouse on the racks and the staff would come in and see me. Can you imagine my old man, trying to put trust in his son? And I'm stinking of booze out of me cake, Charlie all round me lips. Eventually, he said, 'You can't do this no more.' So I jacked and went DJ-clubbing full-time.

TT: When you were playing and travelling all over the world, did you always try and watch Spurs if you could? Have you got any good stories on that?

BB: I always tried to watch a game wherever we was, but, as you said, we were travelling a lot. If by any chance Spurs were playing, then great. If it was in the summer, which it was mostly was, no good, as there was no football. The England games were good, as everyone was out.

TT: Yeah, I can imagine.

BB: You have to remember that all those years back, when I was travelling a lot, Sky [TV] was very rare.

TT: Yeah, shame it came about at all. The live games were special back then; they're two a fucking penny now.

BB: Yeah, it's only been the last 15 years, max, that Sky has taken off, and football has become the massive sport it was, so, if you were miles away back then, it wasn't happening.

TT: Yeah, I can remember watching the Milk Cup final in Thailand just before I was banged up for Chelsea [concerning an attack on Chelsea fans – see page 111 of *Tottenham Massive*]. It was at night and about 80 degrees and pissing down with rain. Surreal.

BB: It's the one thing we all have in common. It's our game. I've travelled all over the world and back. Then, Sky was a fortune, and you couldn't take your card abroad and all that. It's only recently it's all opened up big time.

TT: Tell me about the best gigs you've ever played and what does it feel like to rock a crowd like that?

BB: The best club we ever did was Space in Ibiza, me and Alex, as far as having a crowd there for ya [is concerned]. It was fucking electric, mate; it was mental, such a buzz.

TT: It must have been better than any drug.

BB: Wouldn't say that. Most of the time we was out of our nut. For that split second, when you have dropped a tune, it made the hairs stand on the back of your neck.

TT: Would it be fair to say that you're in a good place personally right now? As you know, I met you a long time ago through a mutual friend of ours at your house. I think you had just smashed your spanking-new sports car into a brick wall. I was well fucked off as I always wanted one of them.

BB: Yeah, I'm all right. I'm a bit unsettled because I'm not in my drum at the moment. But, yeah, I'm fine, mate, as good as gold to be honest. Yeah, the motor I smashed up was a TT, one of the first in the country. I had it repaired and smashed it again.

TT: Tell me about the crazy days, the drugs, etc.

BB: I've met some great people over the years. The mad days, the not-give-a-fuck days. You just get to meet some great people – yourself included. I've had sessions with everyone and they still say today, 'Blocks, come on, let's get on one.' And, all right, some would say it ain't right to be proud of it but I'm alive to tell the tale, all right? It was a bit excessive but it was good fun.

TT: I can relate to that, but obviously, for health and monetary reasons, would it be fair to say you had to calm down your old lifestyle?

BB: Oh, fuck me, yeah, of course, for both them reasons. I can't put in this book what I've spunked. I had a little count-up the other day and you wouldn't believe it.

TT: Yeah, I would, because I have done the same, albeit on a smaller scale, but it's all relative. Makes you ashamed, really, don't it, when I think of my little one, etc.?

BB: Yeah, money you could retire on.

TT: Half the time it's 'cause you have a bunch of cunts around ya, don't you think?

BB: It's all club people, ain't it? You give it out, get some back. You may or may not see them again. It is what it is.

TT: Parasites if you ask me. I've been there, surrounded by poncing cunts. There will be all sorts of people reading this book, hopefully – men, women, kids, parts of it. The million-dollar question: would it be fair to say you had a very bad habit back in the day? And I know, to your credit, that you're clean now and don't touch them any more.

BB: Yeah, I was terrible, mate. I might have the occasional relapse but that's very rare. I don't enjoy them any more.

TT: I know what you mean. Was that right that you was given two weeks to live?

BB: Yeah, that's true. I was very ill, I was dying, basically. I had TB. You take an ounce a day, no food, [and] your body's going to collapse, mate. And I basically got to the stage where I was in too much pain and illness. And I didn't want to carry on. I thought, I'll just carry on and kill myself with the booze. I was doing a bottle of vodka to just get numb. I thought, I'll go soon. But it was too slow and I was in too much pain. The drugs don't work. So I thought, I can't go on like this. So I went to see a doctor shrink, to find out exactly what was wrong. He took one look at me and said, 'Listen, mate, you are the worst cocaine addict I've ever seen and I've seen a lot.'

TT: That ain't good, broth.

BB: The next thing he says to me is, 'I'm telling you now: I can tell by just looking at you because I'm a medical doctor as well. You will be dead in two weeks if you carry on. Two weeks, you won't be here. We can take you in for treatment now – or you're gone.

TT: Fucking hell, broth! No-brainer surely.

BB: So I went, I'm not ready. I had one last mental night, before going in the next day – no point in telling you about that, as I wanna put it my book.

TT: I can imagine.

BB: Yeah, so I went in the next day to hospital. They took everything off me. You have to remember that I was living on a diet of charlie and Rohypnol – one to keep me up all day, and then I would need three of the other things to just help me sleep for half an hour.

TT: I can understand totally how that could happen. When you're flavour of the month and everyone wants a piece of you, it's very easy to lose touch. You go out with a load of mugs, get a few beers down ya, a bit of the other and you wake up hating yourself. Like you said, it just gets boring and you have to curb it.

BB: Yeah, but you wake up and do it again and again until it's too much. Make a cunt of yourself and do your money. If you can control it, fair enough, but I couldn't, and, if I did go back to those ways, which I never will—

TT: Good!

BB: —it would never just be a weekend with me: I'd want

more and more I'd be dead in two days. I'd have a heart attack.

TT: Thanks for that, broth. Brutally honest. Can't have been easy. Or maybe it was. Anyway, if it makes one person take notice it's worth it. On a lighter note, let's get back to the violence. What do you think of the things me and the boys got up to?

BB: I was a casual. When I was a kid I used to knock about with a lot of bods from different teams: Gooners, Chelsea, etc. We were all mates growing up. Of course, it was about the football, but it was the whole scene: the clothes, etc. And it wasn't frowned upon because we was never, 'Yeah, come on, get in there.' It's people growing up, mate; it's part of a laugh. You lot now are like the DJs were. It's a sort of glamorous thing; it's like gangster DJs. You know, they're writing books, etc. Everyone has calmed down. There's respect now with a lot of the older boys now, I think.

TT: Depends who you are.

BB: And a lot of people stopped going in the early nineties, because of the rave scene.

TT: We didn't. That's when I was at my most active and we started putting Spurs on the map. We would go fighting in Pompey, when I had dreads, believe it or not. Then come home, go to the Gardening Club, Covent Garden. We loved a row first, then a club. A lot of 'em came out of Richmond and Berkshire. You're a Londoner, the same as me. What do you think about all these little fuckers, stabbing each other for fuck all? Do you think it's overhyped by the media and the Old Bill, or do you think, as I do, that all that American gangster shit is a lot to blame? Or do you think, as a musician yourself, that's a load of bollocks?

BB: No, mate, not at all. I think it's just a frightening world we live in now. And I think a lot of kids are influenced by the gangster thing, plus what they see on TV now … It ain't safe walking down the road any more. It doesn't matter who it could be: you, me, anyone. We had the best of London in our time. We walked in any club in London and knew everyone, and it turned into a worldwide phenomenon.

TT: There was respect.

BB: Yeah, I don't like the West End any more, standing in clubs. We had the best of London.

TT: What was your favourite venue in the UK outside of London?

BB: A few good ones were Ronson in Leeds, which was my residency; Passion in Coalville, which was phenomenal; Colours in Glasgow in the Arches; some of the clubs in Liverpool, Bournemouth and Brighton are wicked. Each area has its time.

TT: What do you think of Pompey?

BB: It's all right. I played that Bar Bluu a few times.

TT: Best bar down there is Drift. Keep telling 'em we will put on a night sometime. Up for that, broth?

BB: Yeah, why not? We'll sort it.

TT: Have to keep the fools out. Tell us about the best in our city to play.

BB: Have to say the Milk Bar, Soho Square, and the Gardening Club was good. And then Velvet Underground, Turnmills, Ministry – they was all good in their day. All have their time.

TT: Don't forget Aquarium had some good nights. Finally, broth, what's your idea of a top night out with a bird?

BB: A fucking good Chinese restaurant, then home for a rump. I don't like going boozing with birds – it goes pear-shaped.

TT: Yeah, it's hard work, especially if it's a sort and they know it. What can I say? You're a star. Cheers, babe. Everyone buy the man's records. Let's have a fucking beer. Your round!

CHAPTER 10
CARLING CUP FINAL 2009 – WE LOST

I've said it once and I will say it again: I do rate the Mancs – or Man United, the Reds or whatever you want to call them. In my mind, there is only one firm in Manchester and it ain't Man City. Don't get me wrong: we've had some real battles back in the day with City. Especially at Euston, where we had some right tear-ups with them in the middle of Somers Town Estate, where we used to hunt them down as they skulked in the backstreets waiting for us.

One such time, I had it with a couple of lairy little fuckers outside the Bull, our old haunt, and this Manc had a right go, throwing punches at my head like a pro fighter while I was trying to protect my head at the same time as trying to push the little cunt through the Indian

115

restaurant window next door. The Old Bill eventually came flying into us from all directions. I ran back into the Bull and went down into the cellar to hide while the Manc legged it down the Tube. I was fucking fuming, though, and wanted another go at them. So, as usual, we went hunting down Euston.

There were the usual suspects: myself, Tel, P and Weasel, who was a right character. We hit one of the estate's boozers, where they were drinking with a few of their older boys, and for some reason the local Paddies made themselves busy and got involved, so we gave it to them as well. It was at the bottom of a little alley where we had a battle with them that went on for about ten minutes. I looked around – no Weasel. Where the fuck is he?

Next thing one of them is on the blower. 'We've got your mate and we're going to chop his arm off.'

To cut a long story short, they didn't. But they did give him a nasty whack over the head (which he probably didn't feel). He was a great geezer, though, and, after a spell inside for armed robbery, he doesn't go any more. So wherever you are now, my old mucker, take care of yourself.

These days, in my mind, City are in the shadow of the red half. And their fan base has changed since they moved to that weird, purpose-built arena that was a reject from the Commonwealth Games or something. These purpose-built arenas are springing up in cities everywhere like Ikea flat packs, and, with the exception of a few, are killing the atmosphere. It doesn't help that they're normally built on wasteland in the middle of fucking nowhere or as far away from the city centre as possible. And you can't take a firm seriously who have a clown like Liam Gallagher following them.

Anyway, it was a sunny spring day, a Sunday, and the day of the Cup final had come around. I was excited, as I hadn't been to a game for years, literally, as I had just come off my ban only weeks before. A Cup final against the Mancs ain't a bad start, and at Wembley to boot. I was feeling a bit rough the morning of the game, as I had been wound up because my missus was out in Pompey the night before with her mates. It's not that I don't trust her. It's just that the city is full of mugs and crawling with geezers. I'm sure all geezers with birds know what I mean. Don't you think their mates are just a fucking pain in the arse, sticking their noses in? Anyway, I went up Palace and got well mangled with some of my old pals – and fell down the hill at silly o'clock. So to say I was a little rough is an understatement. I was running on pure adrenalin, had the right hump with the missus and was also excited. And of course, deep down, if I had bumped into the Mancs, that would be fine. All in all, a dangerous combination, and my instinct told me that something would happen (and it did).

I met Yo in the Duke of York right outside Victoria Station. I like standing outside there with a pint every now and again, because you get all life forms passing the windows, from the crackheads, robbers and prozzies – who all live in a big hostel around the backstreets next to some of the most expensive gaffs in London (great idea, that) – to the theatregoers flocking to *Billy Elliot* next door (I keep promising my girl that one); and you get some stunning sorts dressed up to the nines for the theatre or on their way to Pasha across the road. And then there are all the office girls in their tight suits.

So there are worse places to while away a bit of time people watching. Oh, and for the girls, there's an army barracks, Wellington barracks, just off St James's Place with 600 soldiers in at any one time. Quite a lot of my pals have served there, especially Simi, who is now fighting for Queen and country in Afghanistan with the Welsh Guards. (Good luck, mate! And keep your head down.)

Yo was already in there. It looked empty from the outside, as they don't serve alcohol until noon. So he was sitting there drinking orange juice. Fuck that! I thought. I needed a hair of the dog – and lively. OJ would just make me chuck and, anyway, I think it's a sickly drink at the best of times.

There were about six or seven geezers in there as well and, straight away, I could tell they were football. And they weren't Spurs. I sat down behind them and one of them spoke in a moody Cockney accent about his ticket for the Manc end.

'I'll give you a tenner for it,' I piped up. The Cockney red gave me a nervous laugh as the others were clocking us. They were all lumps in their late thirties, early forties, probably from Brighton. Fuck me! I thought. This is a good start. It's only 11 o'clock, as well. We walked out once Yo had finished his OJ to suss out if there were any more about. We went to the Wetherspoon's pub across the road. I fancied heading back to the Duke, but, as it was wisely pointed out to me, I drink there now and again and the staff know me. And it's also camera'd to fuck, so it wasn't a wise move.

We waited for a pal of mine, which is a funny story itself, as he couldn't find the boozer, so we decided to head to Wembley, a journey I hadn't done in a long time.

We changed on to the Central line. Wembley is a fucking horrible place to get to, even for Londoners, unless you live there, and I wouldn't wish that on anyone. Fuck knows what the Northerners think of it. But they don't give a fuck how long it takes to get there.

There were a few mouthy Mancs on the train taking the piss out of a few shirts. I told them to shut the fuck up, which they did. I gave one a bit of a shove but they didn't want to know. One of them even tried to shake my hand as I was leaving the train. Fuck off! I spat. I was well up for it now.

119

DOWN WEMBLEY WAY

And so we poured out with the heaving masses on to Wembley Way, the new Wembley Way. My eyes lit up like those of a small child going to football for the first time as I got my first glimpse of the massive new national stadium and its silly arch.

It still bugs me why they couldn't have put the towers at the front of it. But I won't start on that again now. I couldn't believe that fans from the two opposing sides could actually walk up the Way together. Surely it would kick off if, say, you'd got two London teams that hated each other. There didn't seem to be that many Old Bill around, either – loads of spotters hanging over bridges, lampposts, etc., but not a lot of foot soldiers on the actual street. It just goes to show the degree to which their tactics have changed, even in the few years that I was on my forced break. It seems to me that, unless they can help it, they are quite prepared to let you kick the shit out of one another and nick you at home, or at work, or whatever, at a later date. Or, in my case, the clever cunts just rang me up and told me to hand myself in. I fucking hate that! I mean, what's *that* all about?

A couple of weeks before, one of our boys had hired out this big gaff called the Silver Spoon, which is a massive social club run by Pakistanis. He's a bit of a silly fucker but if he can make a few quid then good luck to him. And it obviously gave us somewhere to go during the game. It was also hired out by Chelsea and Pompey when they were at Wembley and by Everton for the 2009 FA Cup final. It was a labyrinthine type of gaff that just kept on going back and up. It reminded me of the old pleasure rooms, the old labyrinth, down at the Spurs ground a few years back. They all seem to have shitty little fronts and it just never ceases to amaze me how big these places are inside. It's like Doctor Who's fucking TARDIS. There was just one problem: it was bang outside the Mancs' end of the ground.

As you come to the top of Wembley Way, the Manc and Spurs fans converge into one and then naturally split up at their allocated part of the ground. Me and Yo were following behind a little mouthy firm of Mancs who stopped and gave it to some silly Spurs shirts who were mouthing off in the safety of their own end. But this was the opportunity that I wanted – and these mugs had given it to me.

'Come on, then, you Manc cunts!' I screamed as I ran in with a haymaker – a forceful blow – which just glanced one of them on the chin. Yo looked at me as if I'd gone fucking mad. And it was a mad move like you wouldn't believe. It suddenly dawned on me that we had to go right round to their entrance to get into the boozer – there was no other way. And, to be honest, even if there had been, we weren't taking it. We had to run the gauntlet, and that was that.

It was as if I had never been away. All the old emotions and feelings came flooding back. And, even though I hate the new stadium for many reasons, as you know, having a running battle with the Mancs towards their own end while this new gigantic stadium looked on was as good as it gets. And, even though I think it's ugly, its size is just mad. Things always seem to be smaller in real life than you probably imagined them, but this thing is fucking big, I'll give it that. So, basically, we ducked and dived our way to their entrance, where I had another go at them. They obviously weren't fielding their top boys, but at the same time they weren't mugs. They were just a bit out of their depth. Mind you, if their whole firm had realised we were right in with them – well, it doesn't bear thinking about. It still took bollocks on our part, though.

We saw the light and the massive steps leading down to our boozer and into the safety of my own firm (so I thought). There was a bit of drama on the door but nothing to write home about. Just a big black geezer on the door who didn't know me, and he was throwing his weight around.

He was a prick but he soon realised he had made a booboo when he could see that we were going to steam the lot of them inside. He eventually came over and said sorry and in the end everything was cool. It was well funny seeing my old mate Eddie in there, and I do genuinely like the fella, even if he *is* Pompey. Eddie is cool, but he just lets other people get in the way of a genuine friendship, which is sad.

After we had fought our way through the cops' horses and muggy doorman, it was fantastic to see people who in some cases I hadn't seen in years. There was a bit of drama, which I expected. You know what it's like: you get a load of spiteful twats saying this and that. But it was all bollocks, and my pal and I sorted it in seconds. I really didn't know where to turn. Everyone was there, as you can imagine. I didn't know who to talk to next, and I don't mean that in a big-headed way. It was just old friends being reunited after a long time. I was so happy for those few hours that I couldn't give a fuck about the game to be honest. I had my back to it for the whole time. I just knew we would fucking lose and, of course, Spurs didn't disappoint in that regard, eventually losing 4–1 on penalties to the Mancs.

Now, I have to clear the air about one thing. I really slagged Harry Redknapp when he was at Pompey at the beginning of this book, and I suppose in a way he has made me look a bit of a fool. But I'm glad about that. I only want the best for Spurs. But you have to say we have the best now, yet it would have been different if it hadn't been for that inspired appointment by chairman Daniel Levy – lucky or not. As long as he doesn't interfere, that man will take us into the Champions League at least. I promise you. It is the best bit of work Levy has done for

Spurs, no doubt. So, Harry, I love ya, stay for ever and let's be friends (but Keane can fuck off).

Oh, before we get back to the final, I just want to say hello to the Partick Thistle boys who came down. I've met them a few times and, while I've been on a ban, they have been coming regularly to games. I like them and they are welcome, and I will come to Glasgow for a night out. I've always wanted to, anyway.

Anyway, back to Wembley. As you can imagine, it was all madness in there and it was good to see my old pals. But, as the final whistle was coming, that old feeling started creeping back.

As soon as the whistle went, I found myself out on the street, it was that natural. I also knew the Mancs had brought down all the big boys from Salford with them. There is a bit of a myth that all of their firm come from outside Manchester and they haven't got any boys from Manchester itself. Of course, this is bollocks. Yes, they have untold support in Guildford, etc., but that's the way it is with football. Now we have support from all over the country. But Salford is a right stronghold, make no mistake about that. I know a few boys up there who run the security on match days and in the city clubs – Marlon, Gary and the boys. And they're not to be taken lightly. So hello again – I will have to have that night out.

Anyway, we exploded out of the doorway. As we were

opposite their end, the road was filling up with the cunts. Bang! Before I knew it, I was fucking surrounded by a little firm of Mancs. I flew into the first few, lashing out wildly. 'Come on, you Manc cunts!'

Amazingly, they backed off. Then they came back at me when they realised I was cut off from everyone else.

Bang! I jabbed a right-hander again, watching my back and moving back to safety. Out of the corner of my eye, I saw uniforms charging towards me. Fuck! Old Bill. I took off like a little sprinter. Unfortunately, I ran straight into another copper. I poleaxed him, then tripped over the cunt (how's *that* for luck!). I scrambled up and went to go again. This couldn't be happening, surely. Four of them literally wrestled me on to the floor and then put the cuffs on so high and tight that I thought my arms were going to come out of their sockets.

NICKED

I was so angry with myself that I was going radio again, giving the Old Bill shitloads. Of course, it's a muggy thing to do and it just winds them up even more, but I was past caring. I was dragged literally kicking and screaming back past our boozer. I was screaming at the boys to do the Old Bill. They just looked at me as if I was mad. In a way, it made sense. But in another, at the time, it fucking pissed me off. I was held in a van round the back of the ground for nearly two hours while the Old Bill cleared the streets.

I carried on arguing, as I had nothing to lose (or so I thought). I asked the little copper I had poleaxed if he was old enough to drive and that my little girl hit harder. He just leaned over and smiled.

We eventually got the green light to move, but not before I was searched.

'Have you got anything on you that you shouldn't have?' he asked.

'Yeah, you.'

Next thing, he dived into my pockets while my hands were somewhere up around my shoulders, and my jeans, with his help, were nearly down by my thighs. I looked like one of those ragamuffins who walk around with their arses hanging out (what the fuck is all that about?). Anyway, to cut a long story short, they found half a gram of the finest Colombian. All hell broke loose with smug 'got you now' grins. I personally didn't give two fucks. I know it was a pony amount and personal and, deep down, so did they. But it was just because it was me. I wouldn't mind, but I never even got a fucking chance to try it.

I arrived at Wembley nick and decided to change tactics. I was captured and that's it. No point in causing more grief. Especially with desk sergeants. In my experience you don't want to get on the wrong side of *them* because, at the end of the day, they control the whole shebang – bail or no bail. That simple. The copper was asked if I had been a nuisance, and amazingly he said no. The sergeant asked me if it was charlie I'd got, and I said I fucking hoped so, which was later confirmed (unfortunately).

While I was being processed, one of my pals, Jimmy, got brought in. Up to now, I didn't think they really knew who I was. He had claret streaming out of his eye and I gave him the 'I don't know you' wink, which was about as good as a chocolate teapot, as the sergeant went, 'Say hello to your mate, Tanner. Bang him up.'

And that was me. Years of banning orders, first game back, Spurs versus Man United, you're nicked!

I've got to say that the sergeant was as good as gold, but the fact is that I still got nicked, and it's still ongoing, so I don't want to talk about it, if that's OK. I just hope I'm still here to finish the book!

Whatever happens, another ban is in the pipeline, no doubt about it. But fair play to the Mancs – I will always turn out for them, which in my mind is a mark of respect.

CHAMPIONS LEAGUE FINAL

I was asked to write an article for a national newspaper about my personal thoughts on the Eyeties getting the Champions League final again. I thought it was fucking wrong, especially with the obvious fact that *their* Old Bill are out of control and just let them ultra cunts run riot. As it turned out, it went off quite peacefully. No doubt, though, there were probably many unreported incidents that certain boys could tell you. And no doubt trouble was averted because it was not two English clubs out there. If it had been, say, United–Liverpool or Spurs–Chelsea (some hope!), then there would have been a bloodbath. But, as they were playing soppy Barcelona, it was a non-event.

They are strange sods, the Spanish, don't you think? They have the opportunity to mix it with all the English teams yet they just run around draped in silly flags and that. But over there, even though they won, they went mental and had it with the Old Bill all night smashing the place to pieces in the process. Very strange. Could you imagine an English firm doing that over here? They would be going on about it for years. You only have to look at what a meal they made of it when those silly Rangers pricks went on the rampage in Manchester. All right, it was a bit naughty, but we all know that they had bods from half of England with them as well, and that it had fuck all to do with the football.

Anyway, this is my take on why Rome never deserved the final. In the end I didn't put it forward to the paper because, among other things, I was just too busy on this book. So it might as well go in here. First is the brutal uncensored version (my version), then a professional watered-down version. See what you think.

MASSIVE ATTACK

THE TANNER VERSION

ROME – EUROPEAN CUP FINAL 2009. OPEN SEASON ON THE ENGLISH
My name is Trevor Tanner and I am an author of the bestselling book *Tottenham Massive*. I have also been commissioned for a second book, which is due to be published next year. I am a member of the notorious Yid Army, the hooligan wing of Tottenham Hotspur Football Club. Over the years I have been involved in football violence in this country and abroad. I am now trying to leave this scene behind and concentrate on my writing, and life in general. I am not going to make apologies for football violence. The fact is that it has always been around and always will be. I have been asked to write this piece on why I think the Italians should not be allowed to have the final. I am obviously overqualified to express my opinion, so here it is.

Let's be honest, it's a fucking disgrace that the Eyeties have been given the final. Everyone knows it is from our government to the Italian government. Our own government is too spineless to intervene; in fact, I would go as far as to say that they don't give two fucks that innocent people's lives will once again be in danger at the prospect of running the gauntlet of the so-called ultras (I thought that was a fucking toothpaste). And the notorious Italian riot police, who are worse than the muggy ultras.

Anyone who has visited Italy for football will tell you that they are just licensed thugs who actually stand by while the ultras are allowed to throw bottles of piss, shit, seats, flares and anything else that takes their fancy. And eventually when the English retaliate they get what they wanted all along, the chance to beat the shit out of every English supporter that gets in their way, not caring if they are part of the firm or an old man, woman or child. Which happened when the Mancs went out there last year – the cameras caught it all. It's a fucking disgrace that our government does nothing but hand out banning orders to its own citizens while the fucking Italians can come over here and get looked after like fucking gold dust by our Old Bill. And let me tell you: if it wasn't for our Old Bill protecting them, they would get fucking battered over here. We know it, and they know it. Take the mugs away from their own manor and they are nothing. But it's all political now and all about money. People's safety comes way down the list, especially as far as the English are concerned.

I mean you only have to look at the venue last time, Istanbul. And it was a miracle that there wasn't a bloodbath out there. It's funny as fuck really, as, let's be honest, it's only because of the foreign players that an English team will probably win it again. Take the foreigners out of Liverpool, United, Chelsea and the fucking Gooners (Arsenal) and they wouldn't have a team left anyway. None of them would get near the Carling Cup let alone the UEFA Cup or Champions League. It's a fucking joke; everybody knows it deep down.

But you can't blame the boys who follow their teams. I would do the same given the chance. The point I am making, though, is that, off the field, all English teams' firms (hooligan elements) will be relishing a go at the ultras, especially the Mancs, who have a lot of history with Roma. A lot of their innocent supporters were subjected to stabbings outside the ground and beatings by the so-called police inside. If I was them I would be well up for the Italian pricks. Can you imagine if Italian fans had been subjected to stabbings and beatings by our firms and police in, say, Trafalgar Square? Do you think we would get a final?

I think it's only a matter of time before Italian police or ultras kill an English fan in Rome, whether it is an innocent person just going abroad with his family or one of our hooligan elements. The fact of the matter is the Italian police and the ultras are in it together, so it's not cricket, is it? Don't get me wrong: if the firms from the English teams going out there want it, then they know the rules. There ain't none.

And as far as the Gooners and especially Chelsea are concerned they can wipe the fuckers out.

But do innocent fans from these teams deserve to be thrown into the mix? I know it is not just Italy where there is a problem with the Old Bill, as my team Spurs had it in Spain with their nutty riot police the day after the Mancs got bashed in Rome. Our firm stood their ground, though, which stopped a lot of innocent fans taking a beating.

But the final is not in Spain: it is in Rome, with the double threat of the ultras and in my mind the even worse Old Bill. As they say, they have previous, so you have been warned. And it is no good saying don't travel, because that's just an invitation for our people, and I would do the same.

PROFESSIONAL'S VERSION

Many people misquote Goethe and say 'See Rome and Die'. Well, the quote may be wrong, but it may turn out to be all too true for some poor English football supporter, if, as seems likely, two English football teams meet in the Champions League final.

Michel Platini may be thinking that there will be no problems and 'everything is ready for the spectacle' but he may in the end find the world has been treated to quite a different spectacle.

Now, there have been plenty of people saying that

the prospect of an English team playing in the 'eternal city' will lead to violence, but I don't think many out there will have such a hands-on, as it were, experience of football violence, or indeed have written about it.

Whatever you may think about the rights and wrongs of football violence, isn't it better to have it from the horse's mouth, or at least somebody who's been there, done it and got the casual shirt? Every Tom, Dick and Harry has had a go at UEFA about holding the final in Rome, but all that has fallen on deaf ears, it seems. As we all know, UEFA don't like to be seen to be told what to do, and like Platini are keen to talk up the spectacle.

But, you ask, what's all the fuss about? The Carabiniere and Italian police will be there, so if anything kicks off then it'll be quickly snuffed out. That would probably be true, if it weren't open season on English fans in Europe and has been for a while.

A couple of months ago, two Gooners were injured in Rome when their coach was attacked by Roma supporters, while another coach was stoned by Roma 'Ultras'.

Before that there was the violence against Manchester United supporters, where they were subjected to hours of intimidation and everything but the kitchen sink was thrown, while so-called Italian police just stood by menacingly in the stadium shadows until the United fans finally snapped and took matters into their own hands and then those riot police waded in themselves.

I guarantee if there are two English teams in the final then that will be nothing. This, surely, is an accident waiting to happen.

Why should anybody run the gauntlet of getting beaten senseless for just supporting their team? And some of those beatings will be handed out by the police.

When Italian teams come over here, I don't see any of their fans getting banned from coming over here.

I don't know of any Italian fans getting banning orders, which are handed out to supporters over here like Smarties; believe me, I should know.

I'm not saying English fans are angels, far from it, and, if United get to the final, then revenge will be on the menu for the night.

But the main reason I'm writing this is that everybody is entitled to an even playing surface, or at least more even than the one at Wembley, and English fans won't get that at the final.

Remember, the Italian police tell English fans not to travel alone to the ground from the centre of Rome because they cannot or will not give protection, but most of the attacks on fans happen in or around the grounds; they know that and don't care.

MASSIVE ATTACK

The Italian police are not up to the job, either through partiality or incompetence.

The final should, even now, be moved from Rome.

CHAPTER 11
ZULUS, CHELSEA AND ME

Birmingham, Tottenham; Tottenham, Birmingham. It just doesn't go, does it? Well, it did one not-so-distant Saturday evening.

The Blues were playing Wimbledon or some muggy team like that, but for some reason they had all turned out in force to have a day out in the West End. Spurs were not playing, so I was kicking my heels. Then I got a call from W, an old friend of mine who goes with the Zulus – the Birmingham City firm. He's one of their top boys and a lovely fella as well. He wanted to meet up, which was fine with me, although I didn't want to get involved with their firm. You know how it is: it's political. I just fancied having a few beers with a mate from Birmingham. W agreed with me as well, so we decided to meet somewhere neutral. Victoria was decided on.

We headed into the West End via a few watering holes on the way. We were just walking through Covent Garden, past the two boozers right next to the station, when out flew half their firm. On seeing us it was backslaps and welcomes all round. I was asked from various bods to come in for a quick drink, as we were heading down to my favourite watering hole on the river, the Tattershall Castle. Well, it would be rude not to, wouldn't it? And it'd look proper muggy. So we bowed to pressure and went in for a drink, which I knew wouldn't just be one. Everything was cool and I was the star attraction.

Eventually, we managed to get away and make our way down the river. Unfortunately, half of their firm wanted to tag along. Well, as much as I could have done without it, it's a free country and, apart from fucking off home, there was fuck all I could really do about it. So there I was in this surreal position of being in my local with half the Zulu firm with me.

A good time was being had by all and I even bumped into a couple of pals (Spurs) in there who I think were as bemused as I was about the company I was in. And I will always remember it, as I had a row with my pal's demented bird over her massive gob. Honestly, I attract them! If there is a nutter to be found, rest assured, he or she will find me and have a pop. Trouble is, when I smack them in the mouth, they scream blue murder and say they haven't done anything. What can you do?

I have had numerous rows with my own people in this way, which I suppose is life's rich tapestry.

Then the atmosphere started to turn a little with their boys receiving calls all the time. Something was up. It turned out Stoke City were in town and were giving it the big one over the phone. I was getting the odd glance, which was really starting to wind me up. They were the sort of looks that said, 'What are you going to do? Are you with us or not?' Well, fuck them! I wasn't! I'm Spurs and I was just having a drink with a pal as far as I was concerned. And I had fuck all to prove to them, or to anyone. I was fucked if I was going to get nicked for Birmingham City. Can you imagine the fallout with that?

My pal told me not to get wound up and bollocks to them if they wanted to chase Stoke all over the West End. I knew he was right, but, being me, I eventually bit.

I shouted to them that if they really wanted it with Stoke then I would show them exactly where they would be, which I did. I went ahead with W and, sure enough, the boozer was packed with bods. All Burberry caps and scarves. No doubt it was a Northern firm: cheap jeans and snidey Burberry. They stuck out like a sore thumb, which was quite appropriate as it turned out.

I turned to my pal and another one of their boys and said triumphantly, 'There's your fucking firm.'

My pal told me to go, and, to give the Zulus credit, within a few minutes, they were all in the boozer. I watched outside at first with excitement, then I saw smiles and handshakes. So my expression turned to amazement. Fuck this – I walked straight in and pushed my way to the front. 'It's all right, T: they're Derby, not Stoke.'

'Are they? I'm Tottenham,' I said to the Derby bloke.

Bang! It's off. Fists, glasses and bottles are flying everywhere. The Brummies backed me up to the hilt. Me and one of their top boys were the last out of the door, fighting back to back. As I was edging towards the entrance, to my horror I saw to my right that my pal was slumped against a wall holding his hand which was pouring with claret.

'Fuck! What happened?'

'I've been fucking cut.'

His thumb was literally hanging off. I grabbed a tea towel to use as a tourniquet. He told me to go, which I didn't want to do. But I knew I had to unless I wanted to get nicked. In any case, I knew he needed professional help, which is what he got. I was very lucky, as I went out of one door as the Old Bill were coming in another, and I was gone, even though I hadn't done anything, of course. I just didn't want to take any chances and hang around to find out.

I went to one of my favourite watering holes down by the river to go over what had been a crazy, supposedly uncomplicated day with my pal.

MASSIVE ATTACK

My mate pulled through after minor surgery to his hand, and, although he was questioned for 48 hours by plods, he was eventually released, as they couldn't hold him for any longer. So, respect to him and respect to the Zulus. Cheers, boys. The funny thing was that the Old Bill were looking for a Brummie with a cockney accent!

CHAPTER 14
AND THE HATRED GOES ON

Chelsea. The hatred goes on. And on. And on. When I wrote my first book, I dedicated a massive chapter to Chelsea, which was only right. I could probably have filled a whole book up just on the rows I have had with them personally, let alone the rest of the firm. From the early nineties onwards, I have pulled together some of the biggest firms to go to Chelsea, which has been well documented.

I look back at the size of some of the mobs we took over there back in the day (or my heyday, whatever you want to call it) and really cannot believe it. The most memorable ones were Earls Court, where at first I thought it was just going to be me and M, but it turned out so different. I did get there a bit early, I suppose: about eight in the morning (I was well keen then).

To cut a long story short, we filled up three or four boozers on the Earls Court Road. When the call went out for us to move, the whole of the Earls Court Road came to a standstill. It was an amazing sight, and instead of diving into the Underground, as most firms have done (we'd have been captured for sure), we walked the backstreets to Ifield Road, amazingly with no Old Bill. We weren't really on their radar that much then. Their mistake was our gain.

We eventually arrived at the top of Ifield Road, where – lo and behold! – outside the Ifield Tavern were our hated enemies, Chelsea. So we charged down the road towards them, and the Ifield Tavern was smashed to pieces as Chelsea tried desperately to defend it with an added sideshow of 200 versus 200 having a running battle. Probably two of the greatest numbers of two firms having a proper row outside a ground with no Old Bill that there has been.

One lone OB car tried reversing into us to calm it down but soon fucked off to get the cavalry.

The back page of the London *Evening Standard* the next day was '200 versus 200, Spurs and Chelsea go to war'. The chances of having a firm that big now is more or less impossible. Obviously it was going to put us well on the Old Bill radar, but it was fun while it lasted.

Another memorable turnout was another meet I called on in Wandsworth town, which meant crossing the bridge to get to Chelsea. We didn't make it over the bridge as the

OB livened up just in time, while we were halfway over it (what *might* have been, and all that). Where we met was a pleasant, almost village-type manor with trendy little gastro pubs and cafés. That's the funny thing about going over to Chelsea and causing havoc: you are playing about in some of the most expensive real estate in the world – quite pleasant, really, unless you happen to have a house near their shithole ground. Probably owned by their own players anyway, or Russians and Arabs, so fuck them. Nice place to have a drink, though (except Parsons Green).

Again, the thing that sticks in my mind was all of us waiting for the boozer to open, which for some bizarre reason didn't happen till midday (surprised it opened at all, really) with us all huddled into doorways trying to look as if we belonged there. This was a major fuckup on my part. I should have checked the boozer's opening times instead of taking it for granted that it would be an 11 o'clock opening, as that extra hour gave us more than enough opportunities for the Old Bill to spot us.

Chelsea were driving around in motors pulling ugly boats through the window as they sped past (typical of those mugs). So, if those bastards knew that we were here, then odds on so did the Old Bill, which, when you are fired up and ready for action, you don't think of. It obviously suited the Old Bill where we were, as the River Thames separated us at that moment. I remember desperately trying to find a boozer nearby just to get us of the road, which we did when we found an old place called the Bull, I think. Right in the middle of the fucking ring road. At least it was open and the geezer didn't mind taking our money.

What's always puzzled me to this day was why Chelsea never came to us. They knew where we were from 10.30 in the morning, what with all their silly drive-bys. No Old Bill – it was perfect. We were not hiding the fact we were there; we couldn't, anyway. They obviously didn't fancy it, simple. They didn't mind making a silly show when we were penned in a boozer surrounded by police dogs and horses just on their side of the bridge. Says it all, really, I suppose. But the size of the firm is what was amazing. As we marched over the bridge, I looked behind me to see one of the biggest firms ever. It literally filled the width of the bridge and the sight I will always remember was the Old Bill carriers six deep across the road with dogs and horses on the pavement. Lights and sirens were blaring and full headlights were on as they came towards us at a walking pace as if repelling an invading army.

Shame Chelsea weren't as game. We were well captured and concealed in what the Old Bill called a sterile area, where we were photographed, searched, ID'd and then stuck in a boozer on the corner. Various weapons, etc. obviously went for a swim in the Thames. Fuck me, but I bet that river could tell some stories.

The point I am trying to make here is that I doubt that

you will see a firm like that again at a football event. And if we had got over that bridge, well, it doesn't bear thinking about.

It obviously hasn't been as prolific with us and Chelsea as it was back in my crazy era, as banning orders and prison sentences, totally out of proportion to the crimes themselves, have seen to that (on both sides). All these things together are a powerful deterrent, especially if you have a missus and kids – or just any sort of productive life. Don't get me wrong though: the hatred I have for these cunts burns in me as much as ever, if not more.

And I have to say that the Old Bill have done a right number on me over the last few years, and that does wear you down a bit. You just have to somehow put it in the back of your mind because, if you don't or you can't, then you might as well pack it in, because, for all intents and purposes, you're finished.

There are firms all over the country (including ours) littered with these people who hang on in there because of the names, etc. Fucking sad, really, and dangerous for them and other people. And, if you ain't up to pushing it as far as you can go, then you shouldn't be doing it.

I pushed it too far early one Saturday morning when we firmed up at the Three King's pub in the North End Road, just in the shadow of their shithole ground. It was to be a fateful morning for me, which would eventually lead to that three-year prison sentence a few months later. This time, because the Tube was playing up, our firm was spilt in half and for a good half an hour or so we were only 20- or 30-handed in one of their boozers in their manor. Doesn't sound a long time but it's an eternity in our world. We were tooled to the eyeballs and were never going to get done at the boozer. And, even though Chelsea sent a scout to the boozer, they missed their chance big time, because, by the time they came around the corner and fronted the boozer (from across the road), with a good 150-plus, another Tube train had come in – and the rest is history.

We stormed out of the boozer, with me leading the cavalry charge with a cosh in one hand and something else indoors. Just as well my old girl made me hand back the machete at my local bus stop in front of a bemused bus queue. The point I am making is the chances of having a bit of fun like that in Kensington are very remote. While the mayhem was going on, the Old Bill were filming the whole thing. And, just like a cranky bird holding a grudge, just when you think it's all forgotten about, they spoil the party and bring you down like a ton of bricks.

But, while I was deep into my banning order, we drew the scum in the FA Cup. It was a few seasons back – 2006/07 – and I couldn't fucking believe it. I was gutted. Fuck it! I was going to be around there somewhere. I did get very close to Chelsea, actually, and I got as far as the Gloucester Road, which is only about a 15-minute walk from the ground, and, even though I was risking my liberty, my sanity and everything that I held dear to me, the chance to have it again with the old enemy was just too strong.

PARSONS GREEN

This was the same day as the battle of Parsons Green, which you all want to know about, let's be honest. This is a true account of what happened that fateful day when once again Spurs took it to Chelsea.

We had no business being over there at nearly eight o'clock at night. What other team do you know that stays over on another team's manor so late at night? OK, Chelsea did come to us in the end, but, it seems to me, more in embarrassment, as, let's be honest, we were taking the piss by even being there. They also had half the evening to get sufficient numbers that they felt safe with, and it also gave them the obvious advantage of getting an armoury together.

So the advantage was all theirs all the way. It shows the respect and fear that they have for us, though. That's probably why it took them so long to come over. If that was the other way around, do you think it would've taken so long? We would have been all over them in fucking minutes, that's for sure. As I said, I was on my way to Parsons Green in the evening, which would have been a silly move on my part. If I had been caught, and – even worse – nicked over there, I wouldn't have seen daylight for a long time, that's for sure.

But, well before that, in the morning, things were also very lively, with Spurs as usual taking it to Chelsea. This is one of my pals' accounts of his bit of fun over there in the morning.

You always know when you are with the right people: you aren't going to move, no matter what the numbers on the other side. We started off by joining up with 250 Spurs in Putney and, as usually happens, it didn't take long for the Old Bill to get on the scene and surround the two pubs we were in. One pub was round the corner from the other. I noticed a small gap on the corner with no Old Bill. Surely they would let me walk through it and off down the road. I nudged my young mate Ben and told him to follow me. I walked through the gap unopposed, then another three mates followed. Then another four and, before we knew it, we had 20 of us on our way to East Putney Underground with no Old Bill whatsoever. We got a call that the other 250 Spurs were being taken to West Brompton and walked to the ground from there. What we didn't know was that every copper was going to be involved in this, leaving none outside Fulham Broadway, where our 20 were now heading. On the way to the Broadway, I had a look around and trusted everyone with me. I'd had a call that Chelsea were slapping Tottenham fans with shirts (as usual) as they were coming out of the Tube. This was still the case a few minutes later when we came marching out. We knew it was time to let these mugs know who we were.

S ran over and gave one of them a slap and that was it. It went right off. P came flying in, then we all went into them together. Within a few seconds they realised we had only 20 and surrounded us, the only thing separating us being two policemen on horses who had come galloping down the road when they saw Spurs steaming in. Any other firm who had a team outnumbered 100 to 20 would be smashing the 20 all over the place. But for some reason they wouldn't come into us and all the punches being thrown were from Spurs who kept going into Chelsea. I managed to get a couple of Kung Fu kicks much to the amusement of my mate Ben (Karate Kid).

Soon, police reinforcements arrived and got in between us. Then, all of a sudden, as if by magic, Chelsea were making out that they wanted to have a go.

S held his arms out wide, looked at Chelsea and screamed, 'It's so fucking easy.' I have to admit, he took the words right out of my mouth.

Later on that night, it went off in Parsons Green, when a mob of Spurs had it with a mob of Chelsea.

Despite Chelsea having knives, bats and machetes (not forgetting the hockey sticks with 6-inch nails sticking out of them of course), Spurs stood their ground and, by the time the Old Bill turned up, Spurs were coming on top. Chelsea, as usual, will deny this but after getting done in previous battles at the Ifield Tavern, West Kensington, Edgware Road and Charing Cross, one day they have got to be honest and admit that they cannot live with Spurs.

Cheers, mate, nice one, and well done. It takes bollocks to go there with those numbers, that's for sure. And to come out of it with a little result is blinding. But this is now the main event of what really happened one early spring Sunday evening outside the Sloaney Pony, looking out on to tranquil Parsons Green in the middle of some of the most expensive real estate in the world. This is straight from one of the soldiers' mouths.

PARSONS GREEN, 11 MARCH 2007 – THE TRUTH

Much has been written about this day and even more has been talked about it, but let me put the record straight: Spurs did *not* get done at Parsons Green, let alone run. Here is a true account of what happened on that fateful day.

As usual for a game at Stamford Bridge, Spurs had a big firm out early that day and this time we had decided to meet at Putney. With it being a quarter-final of the FA Cup, our allocation was a lot bigger than normal, which meant most of the lads managed to get a ticket for the match. As usual with high-profile games like these, it seemed like half of the Metropolitan Police were on duty in west London that day, and it wasn't long before the pubs we were in were surrounded by vans.

The days of a big firm meeting up without plod being far away are long since gone, unless you meet miles away from where the match is being played. I remember one year we had a 300-strong firm at Wandsworth with no Old Bill near us, until we marched over the Thames only to be met by a hundred of the Met's finest.

We therefore knew that nothing major was going to happen before the game except for the usual handbags outside the ground. The difference between Tottenham and Chelsea is that no one likes going to Tottenham (ask any firm), whereas going to the playground of the rich and famous is like a walk in the park. Instead of walking down Tottenham High Road with its numerous boarded-up shops and pubs, with the added pleasure of the stereotypical can of lager in the hand of a local lowlife scumbag who would sell their own mother for a bag of smack, away fans at Chelsea can walk down the Kings Road as they pass

153

the expensive wine bars and restaurants, mingling with the cappuccino-drinking rugby clan who have started supporting Chelsea only since Roman Abramovich brought over his cash from Russia.

So, as I said, nothing of any note happened before the game. Those of our lot who didn't have tickets actually went to watch the game in one of Chelsea's pubs in Pimlico, which is a piss-take in itself. For a change, Spurs actually played above themselves and the recent trip to Northern Portugal to play Braga in the UEFA Cup didn't seem to affect them. To be honest, we were the better team and we should have beaten them for the first time at Stamford Bridge since the days of Gary Lineker, but in the end we had to settle for a 3–3 draw.

After the match, Spurs marched out unopposed (something that Chelsea can't say when they leave White Hart Lane), and made their way in several different groups to various locations in west London. It was a nice day and, as it was an early kick-off, no one was going home for their Sunday lunch. Spurs were spread across different pubs in west London but were in constant contact with each other, as we didn't want to attract the attention of the boys in blue.

By this time, the usual phone calls had started between the two firms with the usual idle threats being exchanged by both. We knew that, if we were going to have the row with Chelsea, we would have to go back on their manor, as Chelsea like the advantage of their own backyard and they probably wouldn't want to come to us. Fair enough, we were the away firm, so it was really down to Spurs to go back. Mind you, since their failed attempt of attacking the Bull (Spurs' main pub back in the early 1990s), every row between Spurs and Chelsea has taken place on their manor. This even includes when we have been playing at home and we have still gone down to them; the Lord Burleigh at Victoria springs to mind (and that's another story altogether).

Anyway, let's cut to the chase. After many phone calls and much marching around London (including giving the Spurs police spotters the runaround on Oxford Street), it was decided that we would go to their manor, find a pub and call it on. Parsons Green has always been a Chelsea stronghold, so we headed there by Tube and plotted up in the first pub we came across which was called the White Horse. Contact was made, so Chelsea knew where we were and we weren't going anywhere until they made their appearance. They kept saying (on the phone) that they had a surprise for us, and we all agreed that it would be a surprise if they actually turned up.

It seemed like we were waiting outside this posh pub for hours. Some of our lot even got fed up with the waiting and went home, as it was getting quite late in the day now and the game had finished some five hours ago. This is a tactic that Chelsea use quite a lot. They say they are coming in a few minutes, then make you wait ages, hoping that your numbers start to dwindle. They even sent a van down to spy on us to see what numbers we did have, and I guarantee if we did have more than the 35–40 who were there they wouldn't have turned up at all, as Chelsea always like to have the numbers supremacy. I could have sworn that this van that kept circling the pub was driven by Donal MacIntyre, but even Chelsea aren't stupid enough to let an Irish investigative journalist drive their top boys around.

Just as we were thinking they weren't coming, the shout went up that a mob was marching towards the pub from the direction of the tube station. This was it. The adrenalin started to pump and everyone was shouting the usual stuff about getting ready. Everyone was half expecting the usual bottles and bricks to be thrown, and then, once Chelsea ran out of ammunition, they would be on their toes as usual. Well, this wasn't Chelsea's usual mob: this was the best mob they had pulled together for years. Their numbers were similar to ours, but it was all their old faces and they were tooled up to the eyeballs. You could see from their eyes that they fancied their chances. This was going to be payback for all the times Spurs had taken the piss out of Chelsea in the last 20 years.

There was a little path outside the pub, no more than six feet wide, and this was where our mob was. We had no tools, except the odd glass or bottle. We had to hold this path, otherwise we would be on our toes and Chelsea would have had their revenge. The Chelsea mob came flying into us, but this time they weren't throwing anything at us: they were battering us with every sort of weapon imaginable.

It later emerged that they had baseball bats, hockey sticks, coshes and lumps of wood with nails in. I didn't know Chelsea had a men's hockey team. This was their big surprise – they came armed to the teeth. They had to, as they thought that this would be the only way they could ever get the better of us. If it was just the case of a few bats and lumps of wood, then this is nothing we haven't faced before, but it soon became apparent that at least three or four of them were carrying knives, and they weren't scared to use them. (Although no one was seriously injured, seven of our lot suffered stab wounds during the fight.)

The actual fight went on for what seemed like ages, but in reality it lasted five minutes, which, as any of you who have ever been involved in a row at football know, is a fucking long time. Both firms gave as good as they got, and, even though we were sustaining most of the injuries, our firm stood tall and we never got backed off, not even an inch. I doubt if there is another firm in the country who would've stood their ground like Spurs did that night.

Once we got over the initial surprise that this wasn't the usual muggy Chelsea firm, we started to sense that they were there for the taking. I have heard since that they actually thought that, once we saw their armoury, we would be on our toes as soon as they turned up. They must have got us mixed up with that other mob down the other end of the Seven Sisters Road. Just as we sensed they were beginning to back off, the first sounds of the police sirens were heard. This is usually the signal to fuck off, as no one wants to get nicked and, as this wasn't your usual handbag football row, we knew the OB would be looking for as many arrests as possible.

I remember that the fighting was still going on even after the OB had jumped out of their vans. There were up to 80 mainly bloody and bruised men running in all directions trying not to get nicked. There were lads hiding in bushes, under cars, trying to flag down taxis, anything to avoid spending the night in the cells. A good few of our lot managed to get on to a passing bus, only for the police to pull it over and arrest them all.

In the end, about 40 lads in total spent the next 15 hours at various nicks around west London. As any of you who have sampled the delights of a night in the cells will know, sleeping isn't an option, especially with the bright lights and constant banging and shouting (and that's just from the police officers). All you can do is think about what you are going to say in your interview, and just pray there were no fucking cameras. It doesn't matter what walk of life you come from, whether you work in a bank or are unemployed, no one wants the hassle of a court case or, even worse, a spell at Her Majesty's pleasure.

In the end, out of forty arrests, only eight made it to court: two lads from Tottenham and six from Chelsea. The only reason more didn't get charged was the fact that there was no CCTV of the pub or the surrounding area – thank fuck!

The trial went on for about two months and I think both firms were content with the verdicts. Only one from each side got a guilty verdict, and thank fuck neither of them got a custodial! Both sets of Old Bill would've seen this as a failure, considering the cost and resources that they ploughed into that day. We even had a drink-up for our lad, who we all thought was going to go away for at least a year – and maybe one day I will get my 50 quid back off him.

One noteworthy thing to come out of the trial was

how one of Chelsea's main lads actually admitted to one of our lot that, if the Old Bill hadn't turned up when they did, then they were about to be on their toes. Unfortunately, they will never admit this in any of their books – which you will find in the fiction section of all good bookshops!

I don't know how truthful this next bit is, but I did hear that some months later Chelsea held a party to celebrate their great Parsons Green victory against their old enemy and they even had T-shirts made up. The former New Labour publicity guy Alastair Campbell must have been employed by them to add a bit of spin to the story, as, if this is true, then any respect we do have for them has gone out of the window. Any Chelsea people who were actually there that night know the score. What will they do next? Throw a late street party for coming second in the 2008 Carling Cup final?

Here is an extract from one of the national newspapers:

One witness said: 'It was pandemonium, I've never seen scenes like it. It was a battlefield in the middle of Fulham's smartest area on a Sunday evening. I was on Parsons Green itself having a quiet drink with friends – nothing to do with football.

'Suddenly there was a lot of loud shouting and

screaming and we saw a huge mob fighting outside the Sloaney Pony, smashing each other with baseball bats and anything they could get their hands on. People were fleeing in all directions, it was chaos.

'I ran off down a street but could hear the rioting going on half a mile away. About five minutes later the police sirens started and carried on all night.'

Parsons Green just goes to show the hatred that still exists between the two firms. And, even in this day of Big Brother and more and more sophisticated policing (more grasses), banning orders, etc., it just goes to show the brutality that they are capable of if they get the slightest sniff of each other. There have also been some very naughty episodes around the Victoria/Pimlico area that haven't been publicised at all, but more than deserve a mention, and, as usual, us going to them. This is just a little taste of things.

What you have to realise with these cunts is that Victoria and Pimlico is their manor, but, after we'd done them at the Lord Burleigh, we forced them more and more south into Pimlico.

We had Chelsea at home and a naughty firm out as usual, but there was Old Bill everywhere, so we decided to go to Seven Sisters. We followed their main firm down to the Tube. There were 14 of us – exactly. The plan was to get off somewhere like Rayners Lane and get all the other Spurs to get off one by one. But, and don't ask me why, we decided to go straight to Pimlico with 14 geezers. So we got on the Tube knowing that they're all there (fucking mad). We came straight out of the Tube to see Old Bill fucking everywhere. They thought we were just a few Chelsea turning up and obviously so did the Old Bill, as they just let us walk straight out.

So we made a few calls and the rest of the Spurs boys were on their way. But we decided to take a walk down the road anyway.

Here's a chat I recorded with one of our top boys.

A: Three geezers walked past us. They were only young, must have been late twenties, early thirties.

T: My age.

A: Anyway they were young by my standards: as you know, I'm getting on a bit now.

T: Still don't look a day over 25, broth.

A: They looked the typical football bods, with all their silly Stone Island on. Doesn't make them fight better. Anyway me and my mate looked a couple of scruffy cunts. Next thing, they turned around and one of them has gone, 'Who you looking for, lads? You're Tottenham ain't ya?' 'Yeah, we're fucking Tottenham.' The next thing, they started doing that silly jumping-up-and-down thing. We took one step towards them and the silly cunts had it on their toes.

T: What a surprise!

A: So we walked back to the boozer we had found to plot in. Obviously, Chelsea knew we were here now so we checked the boozer out for cameras – very smart – and realised there were no cameras inside at all. But there were some cameras outside.

T: That's a bit weird, but well spotted.

A: So we decided the best thing to do was to let them come to us – big of them – so we went inside and stood right at the back. It was a Sunday night and there was hardly anyone else in there. The boozer had double doors at the front and at the back, so we knew we had the back doors covered, leaving the front free for the cunts to come in and have it with us. It reminded me of an old Western I once watched when a few people are in their tin hut or house and all of a sudden you can see heads bobbing up and down and a loud screeching for blood and the place is surrounded by Indians.

T: But this time it was Chelsea.

A: Yeah, fair enough, they're here. So we're stood right at the back of the boozer and one geezer's come running in with a bottle, so he threw it. A pathetic fucking throw, really bad, and it landed about three foot in front of him. It didn't even reach us. Another geezer came in behind and tripped over him.

T: Fucking clowns.

A: To be honest, I just fucking laughed. So we're still standing there, while they both run fucking out again. Chelsea won't fucking come in the front door, so we've had to fucking go to the front door. Now Chelsea were pretending to come in the door. It was a piece of piss, holding the door. So I'm thinking, Did Chelsea really want to come into the door? No, they didn't. We knew this because we stood back to allow them in and they didn't come. In effect, it was a fucking non-event and within a few minutes Old Bill had turned up and grabbed a few Chelsea outside, so we just fucked off out the side door. The next day I heard that they were claiming a result.

T: What a surprise!

A: What the fuck is all *that* about? We've gone over to them and invited them into a boozer, yet they still couldn't do it.

T: That sums them up, really. So the Lord Burleigh before this was very naughty, wasn't it, and once again we're moving to them. Have to give that a mention in a bit, broth.

A: Yeah, the Lord Burleigh hotted them right up, or *we* did, I suppose. You have to remember that Victoria was always their manor, but because of that they were pushed further south to Pimlico because they fucking knew that it was a stop further from Victoria and a bit further to go fucking looking for them.

T: Chelsea got smashed in Anderlecht, didn't they?

A: Yeah, they called it on at a bridge somewhere. From what I've heard their yoof firm ran and left a few of their top boys to get a right hiding, broken legs, the lot. We played out there a little while after and they wouldn't come near us.

T: Says a lot, doesn't it?

A: Yeah, of course it does.

T: How did you get on in Europe this year, or last?

A: We had a naughty one with Eindhoven last year in the UEFA Cup. It was a bit of a strange thing as, when we arrived, probably about 5pm, there was about 15 of us.

T: You like that number.

A: There was two boozers outside the station with the one on the left full of Spurs, so we went over for a chat. A Spurs geezer said to us how he thought this place was fucking mad and there was mobs of Eindhoven bowling about the place with no Old Bill in sight.

T: Set-up?

A: There wasn't a lot of Spurs about then, either. We were told that a boozer up by the ground with Spurs scarfers, kids, etc. had been attacked by Eindhoven. So we told the geezer not to panic; we will get together and have a pop. Most of our firm was still in the Dam [Amsterdam].

T: What a fucking surprise!

A: But a lot of our older boys started to turn up so we walked in a boozer on the other side of the road. What we started to realise was that plain-clothes Old Bill were fucking everywhere. I started thinking it might be a fucking set-up.

T: Don't blame you.

A: At the end of the street, no more than 300 yards away in a shopping precinct, Eindhoven were starting to mob up. And again there was no obvious signs of the Old Bill apart from these plain-clothes cunts. About four or five minutes later, just after our first drink, one of the geezers on the door said it's going off, it's going off big time. We walked out and it must have been going off a few minutes already. At the top of the street, Spurs had actually attacked their boozer. All our older lot had turned up and proper gone for the boozer.

T: Fair play.

A: The Eindhoven geezers were all big lumps, and they were having it. Chairs and tables were flying everywhere. It was proper going off big time. I walked up the road to get involved but what I didn't realise was there were cameras everywhere. The Old Bill were hidden in doorways filming the whole thing.

T: Fuck!

A: So it was obviously on camera. Spurs done well and ran them back into the boozer – twice. So I suppose we could claim a victory. It makes you wonder: was it a set-up by the Old Bill?

T: Wouldn't surprise me. It's exactly what they did to me at the Three Kings.

A: But yeah, that was our old boys' proper little thing. All our main firm was still in the Dam, so credit where it's due. It was a naughty place.

T: Yeah, it sounds it. Big respect to them for that.

NIGHTMARE AT THE LANE – LOST 4–0

T: I was at this game so I'm surprised I missed this row, but, as my pal will explain, it was more by chance. But again we're going to them. In fact, I know why I wasn't there: I was busy having it with Chelsea and the Old Bill on Seven Sisters Road. We'd just been done 4–0 in the FA Cup, so I wasn't happy, and, even though I lived south of the river, as was the norm with me, I stayed behind over there until late at night with the boys. I missed my last fucking train and had to fork out a bull's-eye to get home. But, while we were drowning our sorrows, as usual Chelsea had fucked off like ghosts. There was things going to happen at Victoria that got very naughty indeed.

A: Yeah, we were fucked off the same as you, so we

ducked into the Connaught down the bottom of Seven Sisters.

T: Yeah, used to be our beloved Bull.

A: Yeah, that's right. A couple of Aberdeen's boys were in there and they were on the phone to a couple of Rangers boys who were with Chelsea.

T: There's a surprise!

A: He said to us that Chelsea were still about down Victoria and wanted it.

T: That's fucking big of them considering it's their manor.

A: Yeah, I know. We always have done little suicide missions like this. There was about 16 of us, tops. We walked all around Victoria Station until we found the fucking boozer, the Lord Burleigh.

T: Yeah, I know, it's well tucked away and not even called that nowadays. Probably why they changed the name. Carry on, broth.

A: We saw some Chelsea bods outside the boozer, so we all spread out across the pavement. Fuck knows why.

T: Takes some bottle, though.

A: Yeah, I know. But also they didn't know how many we had. And they had a fear of us, let's be honest. The best we could hope for was they had 50 or so, but if they had more then so be it. It was too late now, anyway.

T: Really, you've got no right to do that, but I can imagine them thinking, Who the fuck are this little firm? Must have played tricks with their minds – no doubt about that. Like two boxers going to go for each other, 90 per cent is psychological.

A: They came proper running towards us, with about another 30 outside the boozer with bottles and glasses, etc. They were screaming and shouting and making a right fucking show. And I must admit my first thought was, Fuck! We could be in trouble here. I really thought we were going to get done. But then I thought, Fuck it! We ain't gonna run. We'll get mullered here if it happens. A few of ours took a couple of backward steps but then we were only five-handed at the front.

T: I don't fucking blame them. At the end of the day you're giving it to them and again, in their manor, and we have just lost 4–0.

A: Yeah, I know. Always the same.

T: Bet there was a lot of south London boys with ya.

A: No comment. I remember a couple of Aberdeen. I remember them coming right up to us, then seeing we hadn't moved an inch. We were on them with the verbals: 'Come on, then, you Chelsea cunts.' Then there was, like, a mini stand-off for a few seconds – you know what it's like. Then, *bam*! It was fucking brilliant. One of ours went steaming through and smacked one of them.

T: Pukka! So you gained an advantage again. That's my trick.

A: It went off big time. We just stayed calm and went for it. The row that went on was proper fighting, T, believe me. No jumping up and down. During it, one of ours got done with a bottle in the boat race. You know him well.

T: Yeah, of course I do. He's as game as they come. Bless him.

A: Yeah. Anyway, he shouts out, 'My eye, my eye!' And someone else said, 'Don't worry about it, it's just a scratch.' He couldn't see for claret, and his eye was hanging out. But he still went charging back in. It turned out later that he very nearly lost his eye over it. By the time the Old Bill had turned up, it seemed like forever, but it was actually five minutes, tops. But that is a long time.

T: Especially when you only have 16.

A: By then we had a running battle with them in the middle of the road and on the pavement. Cars were swerving all over the place and by then we had backed them all the way back up to Victoria fucking Station. Just 16 of us, and in the end the rest of Chelsea had fucked off.

T: Typical.

A: And the only two geezers who were still trying to give it were Glasgow fucking Rangers bods who'd given them away to the Aberdeen boys.

T: You gotta laugh.

A: Yeah, and the good thing was, nobody got nicked. By rights, we should've got mullered.

T: But you didn't.

A: I know, but there was claret everywhere. It turns out that later in the evening they were still at the boozer.

T: Chelsea?

A: Yeah. I rang one of my mates up the next morning, and it turns out a lot of them just fucked off when they thought we were bringing hundreds down. The ironic thing was they had probably the same numbers as us towards the end of the row, as the rest of them let them down and sloped off. So in the end they let themselves down. It was mental though.

EDGWARE ROAD

T: It sounds like your little firm have been having loads of fun with these mugs. I know you had another naughty turnout with them. Must have been when I very first got my ban, and I think I was on the run as well. Edgware Road I'm on about.

A: Yeah, it was just an ordinary League game; it was a lovely day at Stamford Bridge.

T: I heard it got proper heavy with a few Chelsea getting proper hurt.

A: Yeah. To be honest, I think this is why they turned up at Parsons Green tooled up to the eyeballs. We had a good meet in the afternoon in a little boozer, which I ain't going to name, as the Old Bill didn't find it.

T: Wouldn't expect you to.

A: It was a proper good meet during the game. It was on their manor, put it that way. And, as you know, we don't go to the game. I got there quite late and there was already about 40 Spurs there. Anyway, the usual phone calls started flying back and forth, so we said to them, 'Look, you've got to come to us.'

T: For a change.

A: We're only around the corner, we've checked the boozer for cameras, etc. and it was clean. And there was obviously no Old Bill in sight. So we've left them with no choice but to come to us.

T: Good.

A: Anyway, they came around the corner tooled up a little but nothing too heavy. Bits of wood, a couple of bats with spikes. Fair enough, really. We were so full of ourselves that I said don't tell the others.

T: Bit cocky of you, broth.

A: I know, but I was that sure we would do them with what we had outside. Anyway, we went flying into them and they didn't even attempt to stand. Just turned and ran. Obviously, by now the rest of the boys had come flying out behind us. I love a chase, especially against these cunts. Anyway, I just ran out of breath and walked back to where the row had started and there was four bodies just lying on the road.

T: Not good.

A: I thought at first it was four Spurs who'd been done. But it wasn't: it was Chelsea. It was a bit sickening, really, as they'd obviously stood their ground and been battered to such a degree they weren't moving.

T: They've done it plenty of times, but I know where you're coming from. It sounds proper serious.

A: Yeah, they weren't moving at all. Anyway, sirens started and we had to move. We jumped in a black cab to the West End. We were sitting there when my mate got a phone call saying that one of them was dead.

T: Fucking hell!

A: He put the blower down and for a few minutes it was a horrible moment.

T: Yeah, I've been there before. You can't describe it.

A: Yeah, I know. OK, we hate the cunts, but you don't want to kill anyone, do you?

T: No, of course not. But it's a dangerous game, mate, let's be honest, and those are the risks we take.

A: Yeah. Word filtered through that they were hospitalised but thankfully no one died.

T: Yeah, thank fuck.

A: It makes me think now, looking back on it, that this is why they came to Parsons Green with such excessive weapons.

T: Yeah, that's a no-brainer, really, broth. And, to be honest, you can't blame them in a way.

A: But what really fucks me off is over my way they were spreading rumours that we had knives taped to our wrists and all sorts, which was total bollocks. They had all the tools; we just took them off them. We had fuck all.

T: Don't worry about it. I've had that shit from them all my life.

Well, to finish off, what can I say? You have all been busy boys, big time. And this will probably be the last time I write about Chelsea, and I know in my heart that what is said is the truth. It's not personal, and I know they hate me and vice versa. And they probably think that I have a personal vendetta against them, but it's about the hatred between our firms. I've even got a few mates who support the pricks – most bods have got pals who support different London teams. That's the way London is, and anyone that says different is a liar. I do know one thing: it will never end between us and them. Will we be there again, having it? I wouldn't bet against it.

Finally, you're probably wondering why I never mentioned the League Cup final at Wembley. Simple: it was a non-event. We called it on in Ruislip, again, in their manor and, to cut a long story short, we had a monster firm, but they didn't want to know. I rest my case, Your Honour.

WEST HAM

OK, West Ham. I hate the cunts. To me, they are now on the same level as Chelsea, telephone gangsters. I never thought they would come down to that level; it was a surprise and quite sad, because to me it said that a once formidable firm was reaching rock bottom. I'll say it again, West Ham do not bother me at all. I'm not saying that in their day they were not the guvnors, but this ain't the eighties – this is *our* day.

Let's start, as all good fairytales do, at the beginning. Once upon a time in the 1980s, there was a little firm called the ICF. And at the time, so legend has it, they were the best firm around. And so the story goes that back in those dark days they always had the upper hand on us. Even though we also had a formidable firm in those days compared with most other teams, to us and West Ham it was definitely a psychological thing.

The worst thing that happened to us in the early eighties was when we went to East Ham. We had a good 100–150 people, which seems a lot, but in those days it was fuck all.

Let's talk to my mate again, because the story of our biggest mistake is now taken up by him.

A: Our mistake was to get off at East Ham. We had earlier met at Manor House. I suppose we were the Inter-City Firm. It was our time to step up to the plate for the older boys. We had a good 150-plus, which in those days was fuck all. They probably had a couple of geezers on the Tube, so they knew we were coming and it was so early in the morning that they didn't have many boys out. To be honest, I would say no more than 50. And you have to remember that there were no mobiles back in those days.

T: So no warning.

A: What they did do, they turned over a hardware shop so they were tooled to the eyeballs. You had geezers with pitch forks, trowels, paving slabs, you name it. We came around the corner and they were at the top of the road. A few bods trying to make a name for themselves went charging down the road into them. We wouldn't do that now – we're a lot more clued up the way we row now. But, once everyone goes, you know what it's like: it's unstoppable. So when they got to the end of the road, West Ham pulled their tools and cut us to ribbons. We got proper turned over, no doubt. I was only a kid. I was in fucking tears with embarrassment to be turned over so bad. I remember standing against the wall by the ground with the Old Bill round us and one of their faces at the time, I think it was Gardner, walked past and said, 'Yids got up early this morning.' I didn't know where to put my head.

T: Must have been horrible.

A: Yeah, but fair play. They turned up and done what they had to do. I even heard a rumour that they were phoning people up afterwards apologising for using tools.

T: I doubt that.

A: If we had done them then things would have been very different. But we didn't and they had a definite edge over us because of that for a few years back then.

T: Until my day.

A: That was a long time ago, but things started to change dramatically. Especially in the late eighties after Heysel. It had a massive effect on our firm: people just stopped going. Our firm went from the hundreds to just a handful. But that's when people like you came along.

T: Me.

A: Well, mainly you came along.

T: Cheers.

A: And things started to change. I think you saw a chance to build it up again. From scratch if you like. The problem is that, when you have a big firm, you've got a lot of weak people hiding amongst it.

T: Very true.

A: So what you did was get together a few people, a tidy little lot who ain't going nowhere, and it just grew and grew and got better and better. And West Ham probably started to go downhill a bit, although they might argue that point. So both firms started to avoid each other because of their reputation and the rep we were making out of respect really. Then, as I said, came the early nineties and things started to change.

T: Certainly did.

A: We had a few things with them but nothing major. Then we were having it big time with Chelsea and other firms. We had loads of things going on.

T: Yeah, like being banged up in my case.

A: Yeah, mate, I know. But, anyway, this leads me nicely to what happened at Leytonstone. Which is the reason I mentioned what happened to us in the eighties. Because it was such a similar scenario that happened all those years back.

T: So it must have been a special moment for you, broth.

A: Yeah, it was. I had been waiting 25 years for this moment.

T: Yeah, I can totally understand how that could eat away at you. Probably because you know we could have done better back then. We've all had rows in the past when you know you could annihilate certain people all day long, but for whatever reason it just doesn't happen. It still eats away at me to this day.

A: Yeah, it is so annoying because we were fucking better than that. I had a West Ham pal who came to a few games with us: Birmingham away twice, where we got on the pitch twice; and Leicester, where we backed them up. West Ham went there and didn't do fuck all. And this was from one of them because he was with us.

T: Well I never!

A: I ain't going to lie. I even went to a few West Ham games with him. Only London derbies against the Gooners.

T: That's all right, then.

A: But, like I said, he came to Liverpool and everywhere with us. And he couldn't work out why we never did better, as he thought our firm was the dog's bollocks.

T: Would it be fair to say that a lot of our older boys had a problem with West Ham?

A: Yeah. I think they had a problem with them. I'm not sure why, but I think a lot of people will tell you that it was outside influences getting in the way, like business with each other, etc., gangster shit, whatever you want to call it.

T: Yeah, I get your drift. The rave scene, ecstasy, etc. Loads of money.

A: Yeah, that's right. No one wanted to upset them for those reasons. Back then, they were a tight, organised firm.

T: Like us now.

A: Yeah. They could be horrible cunts, knocking on doors, etc.

T: Yeah, I know they like a bit of phone abuse. They must have me on speed dial. That other shit is fucking out of order, though.

A: I know but that's what they were like. More of a criminal little outfit really.

T: Yeah, as I said earlier, no one is saying they weren't a naughty little firm back in the day, but I don't care what anybody says, a lot of it was psychological with us, especially with our older boys, who were there that day. But this is now and that was then. And, like you said, those fellas are all in their fifties-plus now and moved on to other things. Or at least they should have.

A: Anyway, Leytonstone 2007. Bang up to date. I suppose you could call it the lasagne day.

T: Eh?

A: When the whole team got food poisoning from the hotel.

T: So the team literally shit themselves? Sorry.

A: Yeah, that's right. Leading up to that, we went over there in a Cup game and got in one of their boozers with a naughty firm.

T: Yeah, I was there.

A: That wound them right up. And then you had the infamous Cockerel bar incident, when West Ham came over 300-handed at three on a Wednesday afternoon. To the outside world people would think the Hammers had a result. But, if you talk to any West Ham about that, then they will admit that they got run back three times by 30 geezers who were having a drink in the boozer, before coming on top with sheer numbers and smashing a few windows. They still never got in the pub.

T: Yeah, and I know for a fact that after the game they were getting terrorised. I know a West Ham geezer who admitted that, and also I was there. They got run to Bruce Grove and my pal got a dustbin over his head for his troubles. That day must've rocked them bad.

A: Definitely. The seeds were well and truly sown. They must've thought Spurs are fucking mad. We've got 30 geezers just constantly coming at us. They had obviously heard about what we were doing, mullering teams up and down the country. And we believed that we were the best team in the country. And, if you believe that, then you will be.

T: Yeah, I understand, but the fact is that we were and are.

A: But that day at Leytonstone we had a proper organised meet. We was heading for Forest Gate nice and early.

T: A boozer over there?

A: Yeah. Me and my pal went to Stratford first and there was Old Bill floating about even then. So we decided to go by cab to the boozer. But on the way we got a phone call saying the whole thing was fucked already.

T: Which wasn't our fault.

A: No, it wasn't. Spurs had loads in there already, but two fucking West Ham idiots decided to be nosey and check out the boozer, bringing with them the Old Bill. And it was an arranged meet, so they fucking fucked it up.

T: Pricks.

A: And they were only in a boozer around the corner. The Old Bill couldn't believe their luck when they put their heads into the boozer. They had all the Spurs firm fucking captured.

T: It kicked off with the Old Bill, didn't it?

A: Yeah, it went fucking mad. Loads of bods were getting nicked or Section 60'd.

T: Fuck that!

A: Phone calls were getting made back and forth and half the firm was carted off to the nick. And others got split up all over London. It was a total fuckup.

T: Yeah, but not our fault, broth.

A: The Aberdeen boys who had come down were in the West End.

T: Respect to them always.

A: And me and about another 15 were at Liverpool Street, and to be honest I thought the day was fucking over. So we went to a boozer in Hackney to watch the game. Spurs lost.

T: Surprise, surprise.

A: So we all had even more of the fucking hump now. So I got a phone call saying that the yoof firm had called it on with West Ham at Leytonstone and there was only ten of them. And to be honest, I didn't really know them that well. We used to keep ourselves to ourselves and let them get on with it. I knew they were game as fuck, though.

T: Yeah, double game, broth.

A: So we decided to go over there and back them up. The 15 to 20 that we had was good. We had obviously lost a lot of top boys but I trusted them all. So let's be generous to West Ham. We had 30 altogether now at Leytonstone and I knew at the very least we could hold a boozer.

T: It takes some bottle to go to those cunts with them numbers. I take my hat off to the yoof firm and yourselves for going with them.

A: The bit I remember the most was my pal who was standing next to me in the boozer getting a phone call from West Ham.

T: That old chestnut.

A: Yeah. It was a few hours after the game now, and getting later. And his exact words were to my pal: 'Are you still with that little lot in Leytonstone?' So he replied yes and the West Ham bod replied, 'I would do yourself a favour. It's a nice sunny day and the last game of the season. Your yoof have been over here in a motor giving it the big one and winding us right up. What do you think we are coming to you with, a load of mugs? We've got a pub full here, so if I was you I would get the fuck out of there as you are going to get mullered.'

T: Fuck them!

A: Yeah, that's what my pal said. We ain't moving nowhere. They did have a good 120, though. So we got another call from one of the yoof in a motor who was watching the boozer and he confirmed that they did have 120-plus. So we knew what we were dealing with.

T: Like you said, you had enough to hold the doors at least.

A: Yeah, but we had no intention of that. We had a little team talk with the yoof and told them these cunts are nothing, we are the boys now. Forget the past. We've smashed every firm in the country and these are no fucking different.

T: What I've said for years now, broth.

A: Anyway, a builder's van pulls up outside and says to us, 'Don't go anywhere, boys. The real West Ham will be here soon.'

T: So what are they saying? Their yoof firm is shit and can't live with ours? Which is fucking true, by the way.

A: Yeah, I suppose so. Within ten minutes, we spot four

geezers walking down the road and it's four of their top boys.

T: I wonder who that is.

A: By then they had an Old Bill car with them, shadowing them. So we thought, Fuck it! We'll go for it anyway.

T: Might as well.

A: Anyway, the Old Bill just fucking sped off.

T: Probably just thought, Fuck this! I don't want to get involved.

A: Well, it was just local plod.

T: Going to get the cavalry no doubt.

A: Anyway, these four cunts were well confident in themselves, bouncing and bowling along. 'Come on, Yids, let's have it, then,' and all that.

T: Cheeky cunts. I always knew that one of them wasn't the full ticket.

A: So I said to him, 'You're fucking going, don't worry about that.' And those four got fucking slaughtered by the first couple to get to them. We fucking smashed them. They scrambled up around the corner and there was still no West Ham in sight. But as we got around the corner – I think it was Church Road – there was the whole fucking firm. They had obviously wanted us out on the street as we only had 30.

T: *Déjà vu*, broth.

A: Yeah, clever cunts. They filled the whole fucking road – let's be generous to them and say that they had 80.

T: Bet they had more.

A: Yeah, I'm sure. But, whatever, it's going off big time. Us and the yoof just went flying into them. No fucking about, no shouting, no jumping up and down, just fucking man on man, smashing them. I've always rated West Ham but they were pathetic that day.

T: More like you lot were well on your game. Brilliant result.

A: Yeah. They just turned and ran. A few plod started to turn up and they started to come back at us, but we ran them twice: now, and where there was building work going on down the road. A few of them copped it with scaffolding poles, quite badly.

T: What goes around…

A: Unfortunately, when the cavalry turned up, quite a few of our yoof did get nicked. And a few of *them*. I couldn't help going right up to them and telling them they were fucking shit. You could see by their faces – they knew they'd been done. I'd waited a fucking long time for that. It was by no way the best row I've had, but the most satisfying personally.

T: Yeah, I can imagine. You must have been fucking buzzing, broth.

A: Everyone just clicked and went straight into them, no waiting to throw a punch, just straight fucking in. And they just turned.

T: Sweet.

A: One thing that I will give them credit for is that they held their hands up to it.

T: Respect for that.

A: I just want to make one quick point about East Ham in the eighties. They said in one of the books that we had a 400-strong firm over there. That ain't true. Why come out with that shit?

T: Sells books, apparently.

A: It's just a farcical thing to say. They done the business that day so there was no need for that crap. I'll say they had 400 at Leytonstone then.

T: Point taken, broth. Can you see similarities with our firm now and them in the early eighties?

A: Yeah, definitely. What we have now is what they had back then.

T: I think more. But carry on, broth.

A: Yeah, we have a tight little lot who run it. A good tight bunch of friends who don't go fucking nowhere.

T: Can't argue with that, broth. It just goes to show how far we've come. Pulling off strokes like that against West Ham and in their own manor. And, even though the day went pear-shaped with the Old Bill finding the pub, it was through no fault of our own. I was already making my way over there until I got the call and turned back because I was on a ban. I would have been fucked if I was caught, even though it was miles from the ground. But I'm convinced that West Ham probably didn't fancy it that morning and would have got annihilated by the firm at Forest Gate if it had gone. But you and the yoof stuck at it and hung around when no other firm would, and you got your reward. Wish I'd been there with you.

PARSONS GREEN 2 – ANOTHER LAD'S VERSION

T: Where were you that mad evening?

R: We were on our way to Green Park when we got the call to get ourselves over to Parsons Green lively, as the boys had called it on with Chelsea. There was 20 already at the Green and we had another 12 with us. A geezer round my way kept saying Chelsea's old boys were turning up and all that bollocks. We got over to the boozer about ten minutes before it went off. Spurs rang them up and said, 'Look, we're in your manor and we ain't fucking moving.' I don't think they came by trains. I'm sure they came by cars and vans.

T: Yeah, they did, broth. They wouldn't have got on a train with the armour they were carrying.

R: Their reply was, 'We ain't fucking moving from our boozer; we're here.'

T: Fucking typical.

R: Yeah, but you have to remember we had taken liberties with them lately, and our yoof had just done West Ham at Shadwell, which caused riots with the locals.

T: Yeah, top move by the boys at Shadwell, though. I heard that the natives thought it was a BNP firm coming to have a pop, so had it with them as well.

R: I couldn't believe the weapons they turned up with – in fact, I think they went too far. But they were obviously well worried about what we'd done before. They had lumps of wood with nails sticking out of them.

T: Yeah, I heard. Hockey stick with big nails sticking out, etc. Dirty cunts.

R: Mate, six-inch fucking nails. There was claret everywhere but we didn't give a fucking inch. We just stood there having it. But the problem is, when it was going on, the boys at the front were getting carved up, but still standing their ground. We had the boys at the back trying to get through, but it was such a small area, what with the pub tables and benches, etc. In hindsight, we should've gone round the back of them, but you don't think about that at the time, do you? The geezers Chelsea had with them – I've never seen so many old geezers. Their average must have been about 50. This was not the lot we'd been mugging off recently at Edgware Road and the Lord Burleigh. This was their proper older firm.

T: Yeah, I know exactly who was there. They'd been sitting in a boozer all day getting coked up, pissed up and tooled up, and brought in people from fucking everywhere. They had no choice but to come to us, we were on their manor still, taking the piss.

R: Could you imagine if a firm had come to Tottenham that late at night? They'd be leaving in body bags. But nobody comes over Spurs at night, do they?

T: Yeah, day or night. We were over there and it's fucking humiliating for them at the end of the day. We had no right to be there.

R: When the Old Bill turned up, we hadn't moved anywhere. As people were shooting all over the place, we were walking away and there was geezers actually collapsing around from stab wounds. There was claret everywhere. I think we had about six or seven hospitalised. People had been chivved and not realised it. But, having said that, a couple of Chelsea got mullered as well, and from what I've heard, considering we had no tools, the worst one was a Boro fan, believe it or not.

T: Serves the silly cunt right, going with the fucking fools. I know they've always had a little following going with them, anyway. They may believe that by going with Chelsea, like back in the seventies, they would be safe. But this is a different day now, and I bet he'll think twice about coming to London with them fools again.

ON BORO'D TIME

Boro, or Middlesbrough FC, to give them their proper title. What can I say about them? They are a funny little firm and we have had lots of rows with them over the years, and I know a lot of the boys down Spurs do respect them. In the past, I really rated them as I was probably one of the first people to take a proper firm up there in the early nineties, when I took the now infamous 'Londoners coach', the bright-purple one with 'Londoners' written all down the side of it, just in case nobody knew who we were. We stopped to have it with Sheffield United on the way. But, as I said earlier, we got up there in relative comfort, even though it took fucking hours. It was a Tuesday night and we were taking the fight to them.

The reason I mentioned it is because a pal reminded me that, just after we had gone for their boozer on the corner, just before we got to the old Ayresome Park stadium, one of *their* Old Bill came up to *our* Old Bill and they were laughing and shaking hands – or *our* copper was, I should say. He came up to me and said, 'Thanks for turning up – you've just won me 50 quid.'

This still makes me laugh to this day, as they had

evidently had a bet with the Boro Old Bill that we would turn up. This obviously kick-started the ongoing battles with us through the early nineties, which have been well documented already.

Just before my ban, Spurs had Boro at White Hart Lane. And, to give them their credit, they did turn up with a good firm, all in black cabs, which is a good move. The only mistake they made was going into the wrong boozer. A few of them stayed in the pub during the game. The pub, the Ship, was quite a distance from the ground. It's an old black boys' pub where they play dominoes and other bar games, which we don't really use as such, but if firms are going to put themselves there then they are still going to put themselves on offer, and we are obviously going to go for it.

And that is exactly what happened as Tottenham came round the backstreets, came across to the front door, gassed the pub, smashed it to pieces and pulled Boro out on to the road. So that was their 'Welcome to Tottenham', if you like.

The reason I'm going to tell this story is because it has been mentioned in one of their books (which I haven't read, I might add) that we pulled a bit of a wrong move and I want to put matters straight. The fella that this happened to knows the truth and that is the main thing. It turns out that before the game one of their geezers was making himself right busy and getting in right among us, which you have to give him credit for, the lairy cunt. I remember him well, actually. He was a big lump and a typical Northerner. He had a shaved head and I think he was wearing glasses, I can recall. He desperately wanted it with our firm after the game. I remember I was going to chin him there and then but it would have been as hot as fuck and a definite nicking. So we took him for a drink with us. Fair play, he put himself in our hands and we ain't the sort of firm to do anything or make any wrong moves in any case.

Anyway, it was said that we lured him into a trap and bashed him up in the pub, which is total bollocks. And, as I said, the man himself knows the truth, which is the main thing. But what really happened was this. He came out of the ground right at the front of their firm, proper giving it. It was obvious that Boro *had* a firm, as they had obviously all come out together. They were walking down the high street, proper giving it, when they bumped into about 30 of us. We started to have it toe to toe with them straight away, and people were getting launched left, right and centre. One of them, who went down and got proper hurt, happened to be this fella. (You know what it's like when it goes off on Tottenham High Road: people come from fucking everywhere.)

It was now well on top for Boro and, in the aftermath, this same fella was left on the floor. I'm not sure if he was unconscious or not, but he was left with one or two broken legs. Again, my pal who was in contact with him knows exact facts. It turns out the geezer was off work for months, as you can expect with a couple of broken legs. I just hope he has fully recovered for the next time he comes down to London.

All joking apart, I wanted to make the point that what I've just said is the truth. Spurs have been up to Boro twice since I have been on my ban and taken it to them both times.

On one occasion, the Old Bill surrounded the boozer and wouldn't let Tottenham leave. To cut a long story short, the curtains of the pub got set on fire, so the Old Bill had no choice but to let Spurs out. Good move.

It will always have the potential with Boro to go off big time, but, because of banning orders and the obvious distance between our two firms, it has been a bit quiet in recent years. And now they have gone down a division it will be even harder for us to meet, unless of course we are drawn together in the Cup or en route somewhere. But it will go again sometime, big time, no doubt about it.

CHAPTER 12

A VIEW FROM THE NORTH: LEEDS UNITED

Me and Griff, and me and my firm and Leeds United, go back a long way. Over the years we have both been involved in some epic battles. I got a message through a pal we have in common that the big fella would like to meet up with me for a drink and the possibility of doing a chapter on our firms – in other words, a truthful account straight from the horse's mouth about our encounters. It turned out to be a lively and entertaining day to say the least. And, even though it goes against my natural instincts, I got on with him like a house on fire.

We met in some shithole in King's Cross, but I, being the snob I am, insisted that we jump in a black cab and head to Mayfair to have a chat. And this is how it went.

- 1 -

T: All right, broth, good to meet you. This is a surreal experience for us both, ain't it? It makes a change for us not to be kicking the shit out of each other and having a pint instead. I've heard nothing but good things about you, so welcome to London. I would like to pick your brains about our firms. I'll start with the obvious one. How do you rate my firm, or the Spurs firm, to the other London firms you've come across over the years?

G: This will sound crap, pal, but I think Spurs are number one. This is why I upset Leeds. Everyone always says to me, 'Here, Griff, how come you're always on your mettle when we play Spurs?' Because I am. I remember the Old Bill getting hold of me one year at your place and saying, 'Griff, it's a pleasure to bring you through' – then nicking me and chucking me back over Arsenal's manor and letting me go.

T: That will teach you to come over the Lane, you old rascal.

- 2 -

T: What is the naughtiest row that you've been involved in when you thought, Fuck me! This is coming on top?

G: On that bus when you were bullying me. I shaved my beard off purposely for that one.

T: It didn't work, broth. Good try, though. What day was that?

G: It was a fucking long day. It was one of the longest days I've had on a Saturday afternoon. In fact, I think it went into Tuesday.

T: Nice one. Refresh my memory. I remember the bus, obviously, but how did we get to that?

G: Well, to start with, we were out of order. We came out of the ground and I had been in your seats opposite the shelf [west stand] during the game with a good boy of ours, MS. We came out and were looking for the rest of Leeds when it was fucking on me. The little hunchback [Scouser – he's a lovely fella, Griff!] and the geezer with the long hair who everyone thinks is you but is not.

T: Fuck me! There can't be two of us.

G: Anyway, they're all around me shouting, 'It's Griff. Fucking hit him!' Then the one I think is you boots me up the arse. So I clout him one.

T: Cheers, broth.

G: So I've had it in the middle of the road with the long-haired geezer.

T: The one you thought was me but ain't? Fucking confusing me now, broth.

G: Yeah, we thought he was top lad. I know the other one.

T: Thank fuck for that.

G: Anyway, Leeds have scattered, so I've gone into the

middle of the road surrounded. So I said to a copper, 'Here, mate, I'm Leeds and it's bang on top here.' The copper's reply was, 'Well you shouldn't have fucking come, then.'

T: Don't worry, they would've bashed me. Nice to know they're still so polite.

G: So the copper told me to jump on a bus lively.

T: Fucking hell! So we have the Old Bill to thank for that.

G: So we jumped upstairs, and I don't know how long the high street is.

T: Long.

G: But, fuck me, they were on my arse all the fucking way down there. And they were shouting – excuse my cockney accent, 'Fuck me, come on, Griff, where's your fucking famous Leeds United?'

T: That accent was fucking brilliant.

G: It was why that felt like a fucking fortnight.

T: Ha, ha! Nice one. I remember that bus getting smashed to fucking pieces. Someone ripped the doors off. Don't know who that was.

G: Yeah, it was a long journey. You still didn't do us, though.

T: Yeah, whatever.

G: We got off the other end and ran like fuck to get into a taxi.

T: I don't blame you, broth.

- 3 -

T: What do you think is the best firm you've brought to the Lane?

G: The best firm we ever fetched to Tottenham was when we got off at Tottenham Hale. We had a good 500.

T: Impressive.

G: We ended up getting backed off into Broadwater Farm. You know what it's like. A lot of our main lads weren't at the front. Afterwards we got together in the ground. When we came out we had a good firm. The Old Bill had the speaker out: 'Trains to the right, coaches to the left.' So we got an escort even though the police said there was no police escort. We went towards the coaches. We went past the coach park, about 50 or 60 of us. Ricky was our main lad in them days and he turned round and said that if anyone runs they are going to get done later.

T: Sounds familiar.

G: I'm not joking. I swear Spurs were at the bottom of the road, towards Tottenham Hale, so we steamed in. There was a building site so we picked up everything we could and eventually Spurs scattered. The Old Bill steamed in and battered us and put us on a train out of it. We thought we'd pulled a right flanker, and we did. But only because we shit it in the first place when we came out and done a left.

T: Very honest, broth. We've all been there. Anyone who says different is a fucking liar.

- 4 -

T: It's no secret that I do rate Leeds.

G: You didn't put that in your book.

T: Well, I'm telling you now, and I'm not just saying that because I'm sitting in front of you – honest. You've brought some of the best firms I've seen to the Lane, which is well documented. Like the time me and a few boys went into your firm as it passed the Ship thinking it was the front of the firm, but you had brought hundreds down that day. Where do they all fucking come from? I ain't going to apologise for what I said in the last book.

G: And I don't want you to.

T: Some firms you have to rate. You have a massive firm on your day, as do we. Over the years we've had some naughty rows. You have to respect that we don't go around shouting about things from the fucking rooftops. Like, I was disappointed with Millwall when they came to you recently in the playoffs.

G: Yeah, they were rubbish.

T: I remember coming to you years ago and getting a bus into Leeds from Wakefield.

G: Yeah, we knew you were there.

T: I know, I was hoping you would come to the boozer.

We got off that bus, walked over the bridge and there were fucking hundreds of you. We were having it toe to toe. It was backs against the wall. There can't be many teams who've done that, Griff.

G: Yeah, I remember it well. One of our boys, Sean, went flying into you and got chinned. I swear on my life there are only three teams who have ever done that at Leeds. Liverpool were the first to do it, then Man United and you. The only three. You came steaming out 20 minutes before you had to.

T: Anyway, broth, back to the original question.

G: Oh, yeah. You were playing dominoes at the time we came past.

T: Yeah, course I was, broth. You put me right off my game.

G: That's the time the Old Bill were waiting for us and greeted me at the station.

T: That's nice. So, again, broth, where do they all fucking come from?

G: Not just from Leeds. I don't want to comment any more.

T: Fair enough.

- 5 -

T: I know you also hate Chelsea, as we do, or I do especially. What's the history behind that and how do you rate the mugs?

G: When Leeds sing 'We hate Man U' and all that 'Go and get your father's gun and shoot the Chelsea scum' – I don't do that. I don't hate Chelsea and I don't rate them, either, for the simple reason that I went there when they were at their peak, the year they got promoted and they were never fuck all to me. I knew their main geezers at the time, one from the East End and another big lump. We went to Chelsea that year and we run them ragged. And as they were playing 'Blue is the Colour', some of our knob-heads pulled the cord out and cut the fucking song off.

T: Hilarious.

G: We were all over them outside, I swear that's the truth. We run them ragged.

- 6 -

T: It's a compliment to you that you're switched on enough to realise how powerful we are at the moment. And over the last few years most fools outside of London can't see past Chelsea, West Ham or Millwall. Do you boys, or the majority, feel the same?

G: Yeah, they do. I don't tell lies. You can't put this in your book. Like a saddo – like I have since I was six when I watched a Cup draw – I want Tottenham every fucking time.

T: Yeah, I'm like that with Chelsea. [Griff gets the hump.]

- 7 -

T: What's your take on Yorkshire as a whole, on Barnsley in particular? I've met a few of their geezers and was doing a few things with them. But one silly cunt's spoiled it. What's your views?

G: They're Man United. End of. Fucking scum. Worse than Man United. They might as well be Man United's second team. I've read in some books that we are not even the best firm in Yorkshire. What do you think of that?

T: Load of bollocks.

G: Teams like Huddersfield, etc. They're not worth my while. I'm just not interested. They're like a pimple on your backside.

- 8 -

T: What team do you despise the most, and why?

G: Man United. And they can't fly aeroplanes.

- 9 -

T: What team do you rate the most?

G: This is going to sound shit. I'm not saying this because I'm here. It's Tottenham, of course. Which team do I look for all the time? Spurs.

T: Fair enough, broth.

- 10 -

T: What's this geezer Whitaker all about? I've heard he's a bit handy.

G: He's hard as fuck but has loads of little hang-ons. I've been to Spurs and have always been at the front, when we had no escort.

T: Yeah, I know you have broth, and that is when it has been proper naughty down there.

- 11 -

T: I know you have your own security firm, which may come in handy. What's the chances of me coming up there and having a night out without getting lynched?

G: A hundred and ten per cent, because I would die for you.

T: Thanks, broth, I'll take you up on that. You're a gentleman.

- 12 -

T: Finally. What do you think about Portsmouth?

G: They're shit.

T: What reason?

G: Because they're shit. I think they're a bully city.

T: Your round, broth, again. It's been a pleasure. See you in Leeds.

MASSIVE ATTACK

It was a great day and the thing that sticks out the most was coming out of the boozer with the drinks to find Griff standing in the middle of the road with a busker's guitar belting out Loyalist songs. Then some dickhead who thought it was great came up to our company, loving his little show, to declare he was Chelsea. Of all the people he could've picked! Anyway, Griff told him to fuck off because he was Leeds. Then my pal and I fronted him after and said we were Spurs. The poor cunt was well confused. But I wasn't going to let it ruin the day.

On the way home, Tel decided to chuck himself down the stairs at King's Cross. While his three pals pissed themselves laughing, he was being picked up and comforted by a tourist who didn't realised he was fucking pissed.

Meanwhile, me and my missus went for a pint at Victoria, only for some cunt to bang into me in the toilet for no reason. So I went for him and we were having it in a fucking cubicle (you couldn't make it up). I told my missus what happened when I came out. She couldn't believe it. So I'm thinking, Don't come out of this door, cunt. He does. I launch myself back through the doors at him and kung-fu kick him through the other doors. Where *that* came from, I do not know!

All the time the little barman is shouting, 'Leave it, leave it.' So I go outside and chase him down the road, as you do.

Me and my missus went to the rail bar to get the train

home only for the Old Bill to surround us upstairs. We tried to make a run for it, but Old Bill came from everywhere. I couldn't fucking believe it. I was going to bolt, and if they nicked me in front of her I would have lost it.

Anyway, I said he had a pop at me and he said the same. I said I was with my missus, shopping, etc. And the Old Bill were sensible and let me walk – although I think they were more interested in staring at my missus. We got on the train laughing and relieved – hopefully it will be OK.

In the meantime, Griff fucked off back up North to Leeds, pissed and oblivious to everything. Turns out, though, the big man didn't know when to stop and ended up going clubbing and getting poured into a taxi at silly o'clock. Man after my own heart. See you in Leeds, broth.

CHAPTER 13
ARSENAL

Gooners. What can I say, I hate the cunts. Not as much as Chelsea, but despise them all the same. Everyone who follows them seems to be a snidey cunt. Backstabbers. There are loads of the mugs in Pompey. I've had many experiences with Gooners over the years. Obviously, nowhere as many as Chelsea, but we've had some vicious ones, that's for sure. Going back some years, after we had played them at the Lane, I can remember walking down to the Tube station with Big B and, as usual, they were running scared at our place and skulking around with Old Bill escorts. On the way down the Tube, as we approached the southbound escalators at Seven Sisters, there was a little firm at the bottom of the escalators.

'Come on, then, you Yid cunts.'

I looked at B. There were just five or six of them and I recognised one of their boys straight away. They were chancing their luck trying to catch a few stragglers. They must have thought they had hit the fucking jackpot when B and I came strolling down the escalators. They obviously wanted a bit of revenge for the shit showing they had made earlier in the day. They had to be tooled up, as one of them I knew was well known for it. They all put their hands into their pockets and metal objects were glinting in the Underground lights.

We were also outnumbered two to one. This could be naughty. No Queensberry Rules here, and I didn't fancy getting slashed by a Gooner (or anyone else, come to think of it). The only thing I had on me was a fucking Travelcard, and that wasn't going to scare anyone (apart from the price).

I was scanning the floor ahead for something to use against the pricks. Nothing. I looked down at my feet and there was a tin can, so I picked it up and ripped it in half. It would have to do. I noticed that, all the while, Big B was very calm; then I realised why. I was as shocked as the Gooners. He put his hand inside his coat pocket and pulled out a flat-looking object in a leather- or suede-looking pouch. But, as quick as a flash, he pulled out what I can only describe as a mini meat cleaver. Fuck me! I thought. That's a bit strong. But it had the desired effect. He is a big lump to say the least, and he is well used to looking after himself after running boozers for years around north and east London.

'Come on, you cunts!' he roared while running into them with the chopper raised above his head. And I backed him up with a tin can.

They did the sensible thing and had it on their toes. We chased them on to the platform. Not a good place to have a row, let me tell you, as people, trains and live rails don't mix. There was a bit of a standoff and everyone put things away, which is only right. Even though there were people on the platform, no one was in harm's way.

The train pulled in and they jumped on and tried to defend the doorway to stop us getting on. Something flashed by my face. Fuck this! The ripped tin can was smashed into the side of the Gooner's boat, and blood splattered back on to my shoulder. The doors slammed shut and it was over as quickly as it had begun with the Tube disappearing into its black hole.

We've just played the Gooners. It's 8 February 2009. Robbie Keane's return to Spurs and all that. It had to be worth a tenner, didn't it? You can guess what mug put it on. (Yeah, me.) In fairness, the boys played out of their skins. Keane should've scored, his header rocketing just over the bar. A few inches lower and it would have been game over. I don't think Roman Pavlyuchenko is up to it. Don't get me wrong: he tries hard, but I just can't see him scoring enough goals, that's all, which we just don't do. I'm no fan of the little mug, but Jermain Defoe would've put one of the chances away, I'm sure of it.

Why I'm bothering to write about the game is down to Arsène Wenger, the Gunners' manager. Talk about seeing things from one perspective only. He might have got away with that years ago, when his teams responded to all his mind games. Same old Gooners: dirty cunts trying to break Luka Modric's legs. But Wenger didn't see anything. What does he watch, then? It's good that *we* have finally got a manager in Harry Redknapp who will stand up to them. Redknapp said what the whole country thought: he must have been watching another game because we were all over them. End of.

Off the field it was the same old story: 40 Gooners turning up with an OB escort. Pathetic. Why bother our boys trying to get to them? There was more fighting going on in the boozers afterwards with each other.

Last season, in 2007/08, the boys had the Gooners in the Cup at the Lane and we lost – as usual. We called it on with them after the game. So everyone got down a pub near King's Cross – down the Grays Inn Road, actually, but I won't mention the name of the boozer, obviously, as it was a bit recent. It was called on and they were told we had no more than 50–60, so to bring the same numbers or not to bother (as if they would). It was around six o'clock and still no sign of them. Our firm were so keen to get at them that earlier in the afternoon they actually climbed over a wall down Tottenham, as the front of the boozer was surrounded by Old Bill, then jumped into taxis to King's Cross. Now remember: we were at home and by rights shouldn't have to go anywhere. If they had anything about them, they would come to us, or should I say they *should* come to us? They're the rules.

But, as usual, we have gone out of our way, again, to have a piece of them. It got to seven o'clock and still no sign of them. The boys were getting restless now, as they had been waiting for well over an hour. That may not sound like a long time in the everyday scheme of things, but, if you're waiting for a row with another little firm, then it's an eternity, believe me. I would've started to smell a rat by now, but the boys are too game for their own good sometimes.

By 7.30, they were now taking the fucking piss, and you can't blame a lot of the boys, especially with the Gooners' track record for turning up, which is pretty well non-existent – unless they have got silly numbers, of course, the cowardly cunts. Anyway, it's pretty obvious to me, looking at it from the outside, that they must have had someone watching the boozer and were waiting till three-quarters of our boys had fucked off before feeling brave enough to make an appearance. Similar tactics to what Chelsea tried to use on me at the Kings Head, North

End Road. Except, as you probably know, they came well unstuck, as, by the time their little spy had scurried back to them to tell them to hit the boozer now, as it was only me and about 20 more, another Tube had come in with a good 50 on board.

So, as you can imagine, to say they got the shock of their lives is an understatement. Mind you, so did I when my door was booted in by Chelsea Old Bill a few weeks later. Anyway, I digress (big word).

By eight o'clock, there were only 15 or 16 of our firm left. As I said, you can't blame a lot of the boys for fucking off. What with the Gooners' track record for a no-show and the added present threat of being captured by Spurs plod, Section 60'd, then forced to spend your Saturday night in a shitty boozer at the Cross; or, even worse, if the Old Bill have got the hump, a night in the cells. There were a few good boys left, though, as game as fuck. But, if the Gooners turned up now, firm-handed, it wouldn't take a genius to work out that they would be bang in it.

And that's exactly what the snidey fuckers did. My pals Turkish and Craig were outside and told me a bus went by. They thought nothing of it until 60 or 70 boys came steaming off of it tooled up to the eyeballs, heading straight for them and the boozer. Fair play to them: they went straight back into them, and I've seen a mobile-phone video to prove it. Fuck knows who was filming it.

MASSIVE ATTACK

It never ceases to amaze me how these things get filmed while in the middle of a fucking battle. I was told it was filmed by some bird from inside the boozer; who she was, fuck knows.

Anyway, Turkish described it to me like being run over. There were just too many. A few people got a dig and a few windows got hurt but nothing major. I suppose the Gooners will try to claim it as a result and I suppose technically it was. I was fucking fuming when I found out, especially when I heard that we had phoned them up, told them exactly how many numbers and what time to meet and so forth. And, considering it was mainly our yoof firm, the cunts must have thought it was Christmas. Obviously, they turned up with 70 gorillas in their thirties and forties, tooled up. So, if they are happy with that – and, knowing the sad pricks as I do, they probably will be – then good luck to them.

I shall probably get a bit of stick for putting this in the book. But this book has to be true to the last one, and I'm not going to go down the same route as certain other books I could mention that go into the realms of fantasy and never get turned over – as if they are superhuman. That's not right. The Gooners know the truth. On our day, with a proper firm with even numbers, we would fucking annihilate them, as we have for years.

This is a view from back in the day to the present time from one of my best pals, T.

I've always hated Arsenal. All Spurs do. But not all Spurs fans had been battered as a 13-year-old. I had been to Spurs versus Brighton at White Hart Lane when we were in the Second Division. I had gone on my own, as none of my mates fancied it, and I had spent the whole game in the Shelf watching wave after wave of Spurs boys attacking the Brighton boys in the visiting end. It was rare for visiting teams to be given the whole Park Lane standing area, but this just made it easier for Spurs to get in with them and attack them at every chance.

You could always guarantee, when anyone came to White Hart Lane with a mob, that Spurs would get into their end and steam into them. I felt well safe in the Shelf, singing 'Tottenham aggro, Tottenham aggro' along with thousands of others, not knowing that in a few hours I would receive the worst kicking of my young life.

The game was shit and ended 0–0, and, as I left the ground on this cold November night, all I wanted to do was to get home. I got a number 3 bus to Alexandra Palace, where it would be a short walk through to Muswell Hill and then a 20-minute walk from there.

Everything seemed to be going to plan until the bus pulled in at Wood Green, where most of the Spurs fans got off. I noticed a group of skinheads got on, about 15 of them. I remember thinking, I hope they're Spurs, or I'm in trouble. There were only three of us left on the top deck of the bus, all with colours, so there was no hiding place. My heart started beating faster as they walked up the stairs and, as they got to the top, my worst fear was answered with the chant, 'We hate Tottenham, we hate Tottenham, we are the Tottenham haters!'

They sat all around us giving us no way out. They had a big black guy with them who turned out to be Denton, one of their top boys at the time (who is now dead). The Spurs boy in front of me must have known him, as he asked Denton if it was all right for a squeeze. His reply was, 'Go now and you're safe; stay and you're battered.'

As he got up to go, the other Spurs boy made a run for it and, apart from a few kicks up the arse, he managed to get away. That left me on my own. The youngest one of them walked up to me and spat at me and called me a dirty Jew. They all started singing, 'Tottenham's going to die at the testimonial.' They were referring to the testimonial coming up the next Tuesday for the Arsenal player Simpson. The Arsenal geezer sitting next to me, who seemed to be the oldest, asked, 'You're scared, aren't you?' I replied yes. And for some strange reason he said to Denton that they should let me go. Denton replied, 'Fuck off! He's a dirty Yid.'

Then the young one, who was only a couple of years older than I was, tried to impress the others and steamed into me with a flying head butt that caught me full on in the face. I thought it was time to run for it. As I got up, I got kicked right in the bollocks by the biggest one with steel toecaps on. This put me straight on the floor and I thought I was going to die.

Everything seemed to be happening in slow motion but every kick was full force and hurt so much. After a minute, but which seemed like an hour, the oldest one said he'd had enough, pulled me away and threw me down the stairs. The driver, who must have known what was going on but was too scared to do anything, opened the doors and I fell out on to the floor of a freezing cold night in Crouch End. I sat up on the pavement with blood running from my nose and mouth on to my white Spurs shirt, shaking like a leaf. I had missed my stop by a fair few and I was dizzy and in pain from all the kicks I had received.

I started walking back towards Muswell Hill, and stopped to buy a bottle of water to clean my bloodied face. I finally got home about an hour later, having stopped again a couple of times to be sick. Whether it was the kicks to the bollocks, the kicks to the ribs or the shame of being beaten up by Gooners, I do not know, but sick I was – all over the pavements of Muswell Hill.

Getting home, I had to run the gauntlet again, this time from my mum shouting how I was never going to football again, and then breaking down into tears. What surprised me was my reaction. I swore to her that I was never going to Spurs again and I meant it. This was to be the first, and last, time I'd ever say those words. Two days is a long time in football, and by Monday morning at school all my Spurs mates and their older brothers were talking about going to Highbury for the testimonial. I was a little apprehensive but agreed to it anyway, and by the time Tuesday evening came around I was buzzing.

We met at Arnos Grove and we had a proper good little firm: my mate Ricky T, my best mate Rob and Ricky T's brother Steve, who was as hard as fuck and had loads of mates with him who could all have a row. The word was that Tottenham were going to take Arsenal's end of the North Bank, so when we came out of Arsenal Station it was straight into the North Bank.

I was a nervous wreck. It was only three days before this that I'd been battered, and I still had the black eyes and bruised body to show for it. I can't explain the relief I felt when we got on to the terraces and were among thousands of Spurs fans. Tottenham had gone in there in force and took three-quarters of the end. Every few minutes the chant went up of 'Oh, we're the barmy Tottenham army', and 8,000 Spurs thugs would push towards the Gooners with the police lines fighting for dear life to protect the humiliated Gooners.

By the end of the game, Spurs had nearly all of the end, with all the Gooners squashed up in one corner. This for me was the night when I grew up from being a battered 13-year-old schoolboy to someone who would be there every time the Spurs firm confronted the Gooners.

I didn't have to wait long. By the end of January, Spurs had been knocked out of the FA Cup and were due to play Luton in a Second Division League game. I got down to King's Cross early with my brother, only to find out the game had been called off. There was about a thousand Spurs fans there, pissed off with nowhere to go. That was until a shout went up.

'Fuck it, let's go to Arsenal!' They were at home to Walsall in the fourth round of the FA Cup. So, by 12 o'clock, this massive army of Spurs were running around the streets of Highbury smacking Gooners and smashing pubs. By two o'clock, I had disappeared, as I wasn't going to waste my money paying to get into that shithole, but the Spurs who did stay took a good little mob into the North Bank and another mob into Arsenal's bit of the Clock End.

The season ended with Spurs gaining promotion

with a 0–0 draw at Southampton. I was one of the thousands in the Spurs end going mental when the final whistle went. I also enjoyed watching Spurs battling in the Southampton end all through the game, and, to top it all, West Ham got relegated as well. I remember Spurs getting in the faces of a little mob of West Ham at Waterloo when we got back and mugging them right off.

The next season came along and I was buzzing about Spurs going into the North Bank again, although we had to wait until 10 April. By the time it came around, I was 15, and, like nigh on every other 15-year-old, I thought I could take on the world. I got in the North Bank with my little firm of Spurs mates, but it was about two o'clock and there were Gooners everywhere.

Some Gooner, slightly older than me, came up and asked if we were Yids. I said no, we were Barnet fans. And he said the Yids were going to get battered in here today. I remember thinking, Where are Spurs? Fifteen minutes later, I got my answer: a mad little firm of Spurs went right into the middle and flew in first into the lot of them. All of a sudden, the roar of 'Tottenham, Tottenham!' went up all around us and Spurs appeared from the front, back and sides, all steaming into the Gooners. I took my chance to hit matey, the one I'd told I was a Barnet fan, with a flying head butt and told him nobody batters Spurs. Prick.

He went over and got trodden on by everyone else. Within two minutes, Spurs had taken half the North Bank. This is what I had waited a year and a half for. By the final whistle, there must have been thousands of Spurs in there. As usual, the team let us down and we lost 1–0. But we continued the fight afterwards round the streets of Highbury and Finsbury Park.

The following season, Arsenal decided they'd had enough of Spurs taking their fans' home end so they printed little red vouchers and gave them out to fans attending the game prior to the Spurs game. Spurs managed to get hold of a couple and then printed up thousands more. They were getting sold for 50p each, so I bought a load up for me and my mates. You can imagine the Gooners' surprise when they thought they were safe, then thousands of Spurs came flying into them 20 minutes before kick-off. This went on for the next few seasons until Arsenal put up fences to divide the end into four sections, which made it impossible to get the numbers in there that we had been in with. It also became easier for the Old Bill to nick people, so by 1984 our assault on the North Bank had finished.

By the late eighties, Arsenal had decided to put seats in, so in the last game, when it was still standing, which I think was 1989, it was our last chance to get in there.

We arranged to meet at the Fishmongers Arms in Wood Green, and, to be honest, it wasn't a good turnout and we ended up with just 50. I still wanted to go for it, so it was on to the Piccadilly Line and straight over to Arsenal. We split into twos and threes, queued up with the Arsenal fans and met up inside the North Bank.

We had a bit of an argument with one another because I wanted to have a go at the centre, where all the mouthy fuckers were singing anti-Tottenham songs, but one of the others wanted to have a go at the left-hand side, where he said most of their boys went. I lost the argument, so left-hand side it was. As more and more Gooners came into the ground, we got split up with me and the Cambridge Spurs towards the middle of the side and all the rest at the back. We noticed a little firm of Arsenal blacks moving in behind us and they must have known we were Spurs, because, within a few seconds, they started talking really loud. 'We know Spurs are in here. When we find them we're going to cut them to pieces.' This shit went on for about ten minutes before they started pushing into us.

By now it was 2.45. I nodded to my Cambridge mate Richie and said it was time to kick off. He

221

turned round and confronted them. 'Who are you pushing?' I followed up with, 'Yids are here,' then smacked one of them right on the nose, then we flew into them. Gooners came from everywhere and the Spurs from the back came running down to join us. We could hear the roar from the thousands of Spurs in the Clock End: 'Tottenham aggro, Tottenham aggro, hello, hello, Tottenham aggro,' which gave all of us a buzz.

A massive gap opened up with 50 Spurs trading punches with hundreds of Gooners, but within a minute Old Bill had turned up and walked us around the pitch with coins and beer flying at us from the Gooners in the side stand. I got a smack from a police baton for telling George Graham and Graham Rix they were a pair of cunts as I walked past their dugout. The police took us to the corner of the Clock End to eject us, and the copper who had me got hit with a flying plastic pint of lager. When he turned around to wave his fist at the culprit, I took my chance to run up on to the Clock End terraces, where loads of Spurs hid me from the Old Bill.

Back in the Bull in Tottenham later on, we all agreed that we had done our best to leave our mark on the North Bank. We had closed the chapter on something that had been done since the early seventies by all the top Spurs boys before us.

I continued my battles with Arsenal at every chance and, after one quiet game at Highbury, I got a call from a Gooner to say they had done 15 Spurs at the Duke of Edinburgh and had now moved on to the Blackstock. I was back in the Cockerel bar in Tottenham surrounded by loads of shirt-wearing barmies, but also about 30 of my close Spurs pals, who would have a tear-up with anyone. I told everyone what had happened to the 15 Spurs and that I wanted to pay the Gooners in the Blackstock a visit. My 30 mates were well up for it and, to my surprise, so were about 80 of the barmies. A couple of us told them that if they came with us then there was no backing off. They were happy with that, so the next thing you know there are more than a hundred of us on a number 279 bus on our way to Finsbury Park. As soon as we saw the Blackstock I gave the Gooner a call. He answered.

'Where the fuck are you?'

'Can you see that 279 bus coming towards you? Can you see it stopping? And can you see the doors opening?' Then I hit him with my favourite catchphrase: 'Yids are here!'

The phone went dead and off the bus came over a hundred drunk and angry Yids steaming straight into the Gooners. They were getting smacked all over the place until a few vanloads of riot police turned up and started to go into us. But the damage had already been done, and the Gooners had paid for doing 15 Spurs and claiming a result.

The season after, just to piss them off again, I got everyone to meet in the park outside Manor House at 9.30am. I had a good turnout of about 80 and the idea was to take the Blackstock over at 11 before the Gooners could get in there, as it was their main pub at the time. We had people sitting on park benches, people in bushes, people leaning up against trees and people sitting on the grass. To my surprise, the Old Bill never clocked it, so, by 10.55am, we made our move and started to walk towards the Finsbury Park entrance.

By the time we got to the entrance, the walk had turned into a jog. We came out of the park right on to the Blackstock. We hit both doors and there was already a small firm of Gooners, but we gave them a squeeze. As they looked scared stiff, we let them disappear out of the door. Someone stuck a Spurs flag up on the window and the pub was ours. The Gooners later tried to make out they were going to meet in the Finsbury Park Tavern next door. What a load of shit! The Blackstock was your pub at the time and we took it.

END OF STORY

CHAPTER 14
SPURS VERSUS WISLA, KRAKÓW

I've had to break off from my last piece while this is fresh in my head. It's a Thursday night and the sun has come out to play. A Cup night at the Lane. Magical.

Now this Polish firm had been making noises about coming to us for a few weeks leading up to the game. This was Poland's top firm, reportedly, and I had it on good information that it was true, that all the sausage rolls were definitely turning up – and in numbers. The silly cunts at Tottenham had been selling them blocks of tickets all over the ground, as the tickets were on general release and the Poles were giving out London addresses left, right and centre. I bet that, if I had turned up, though, I would have been told to fuck off.

I was going to go over to the Lane itself and have a pop

at them, watch the game and meet all the boys again. I knew that the Old Bill would be out in force, though, and would be protecting the Poles, and, to be honest, I didn't fancy getting pulled over every two minutes or getting nicked for these mugs. So I decided to go up the West End with a couple of my pals to watch the game and see who was about. In hindsight, with my track record of getting nicked in the West End, it probably wasn't the wisest of moves. But fuck it! I was a free man and I couldn't let the Old Bill ruin my life.

My two pals pissed off over to the Lane leaving me on my jacks. I ended up down Carnaby Street, via Victoria, a couple of stops on the Tube, and then to Oxford Circus.

I know from experience that a lot of foreign firms like to muck around about these touristy-type areas, as you've got Soho around the corner with Carnaby Street itself sandwiched between Oxford Street and Regent Street. So it caters for all tastes, if you get my drift. As only a few years before we literally bumped into Feyenoord's firm from Rotterdam, having a stroll down Regent Street, and Birmingham before that. Gooners, Mancs, you name it. So, for me, personally, it had been quite a happy hunting ground.

My pal told me that the Poles were meeting at Trafalgar Square. That sounded a bit too hot for me, though. And, if they were, it would probably be their shirts and assorted mugs. I ended up in O'Neill's right on the corner of Carnaby Street, at the start of the street, opposite Liberty's department store.

I'd had a scout about, round the back streets, Newburgh Street, etc., where there is a nice little boozer called the White Horse. But it was just full of suits and couples having a booze after work and enjoying the last throes of a shit summer. I had one and fucked off.

It was approaching kick-off time and the game was live on that muggy Setanta Sports channel – don't get me started on them. Only 3 million people could watch one of England's biggest games (against Croatia) and there weren't even highlights shown. So unless you were one of the few fools who used to give Setanta your dough and you couldn't find an obscure little boozer showing it, then you were fucked. Anyway, it's gone now, into administration, as of June 2009.

I managed to find a boozer (well, someone had to) before I went to have another nose about. I went into O'Neill's, as I noticed they had the football on and asked if they would put the game on for me, which they did. There was a game on before – I think it was the Pompey game – and, even though I was in central London, there didn't look to be a lot of interest in the Spurs match. But the geezer behind the ramp put the big screens on without any fuss or drama when I asked, which was appreciated. You know what it's like: you stroll into a boozer advertising the game and, because there may be only one man and his dog in the boozer, some jumped-up cunt behind the bar can't be bothered to put the game on. Fair dos: this one did.

I remember when I went into a boozer up on the river to watch the Spurs-versus-Pompey game. It's a bit pricier, but it's the sort of boozer that is fine to watch the game in with a sort. We watched the first half in Doggets, which is a typical sports-bar type of gaff. But, again, a decent place to watch it with a girl. It was bad enough that Spurs were playing like cunts, and of course Campbell, Defoe, etc. were on fire. My missus was pissing herself next to me, so I wasn't best pleased.

Thank fuck I'd changed my mind and hadn't stayed in Pompey, as I was there the night before and had a top night out, bumping into an old friend of my uncle's who now has a bar in the area. I hadn't seen him for 20 years, not since I last worked for him. So Ernie – one of the top boys of the 6.57 Crew, the Pompey boys, whose name is taken from the time the train would leave from Portsmouth for London – and I, along with Ernie's missus and mine, talked shit and got happily pissed.

I love nights like that, don't you, when you can just relax and let your guard down (which is very hard for me). OK, you may talk bollocks (as my missus likes to remind me) but when you get two bods from different firms who you get on well with, and you're with your girls in a nice atmosphere with booze flowing, then there's no harm done, really, is there, to blow off a bit of steam and get to know people. I enjoyed myself, anyway. This was in spite of the fact that we were humiliated on the field by those bastards, who're not even fit to wear the shirt. I gave my ticket to my little cousin, who was looked after by Ernie and the 6.57 boys all day. So I have to say thanks for the hospitality all weekend, broth.

Anyway, let's get back to London. Me and my missus strolled into the boozer for the second half only to find no football on, with some silly cunt sitting down on his own playing on his laptop and watching the motor racing (the fucking nonce). I asked the barman to turn it back over but he was having none of it, so I told the geezer to fuck off home and watch it. But I then got dragged out by my missus before I could make a fool of myself. So we went back to Doggets and watched the mugs play out the second half there.

The final score: Portsmouth 1, Spurs 0, with those two Judas scum having a blinder. I put Defoe in with Campbell as well. He's a horrible little cunt, and I can't understand why he got such a good reception as he did at Fratton Park, Portsmouth's stadium. It made me sick, actually. Pompey is his level, simple as that. He ain't England class and will get found out sooner or later. He is only doing well at the moment because of Harry Redknapp. And, as for Campbell, fuck him. What a wanker.

As I'm writing this Spurs are bottom of the table after seven games. 'The last time we were this bad', scream the headlines, 'is when the *Titanic* sank.' Just my luck to be supporting Spurs when they are so fucking shit.

SUNDAY, 19 OCTOBER 2008: STOKE CITY 2, SPURS 1

Yeah, it's got that bad. And, to be honest, it was to be expected. Or put it this way: I expected it. Sadly, we haven't got the right to go to even the Stokes of this world and get a result. I know it is early days and all that bollocks, but I really think we could be going down. Now I know that everyone has got an opinion on it all, but the chairman Levy and that Damien Comolli have got to take a lot of the blame. But so have the shitbag players: they have got to stand up and be counted.

Back to the Poles. So, I was now plotted up in Carnaby Street and I couldn't find any Poles to write home about, which is fucking hard in London, as you are usually tripping over them. There were a few Spurs bods in there who were drifting past, but on the whole everyone was at the Lane. There were also a few West Ham old boys in there who, I have to admit, were as good as gold and even bought me a drink – apart from the geezer in the snide red sports top who nearly got a clump, which would have been embarrassing, as it turned out to be a Liverpool top.

MASSIVE ATTACK

It was all peace and love in the boozer and I got pissed with my new pals for the night.

However, over at the Lane, it was a different story and all sorts of mayhem was breaking out. The Poles turned up with what I've been told was one of the biggest firms ever seen at the lane. A good 800-strong.

And, as soon as they got out at Seven Sisters, they started playing up with the Old Bill, which, down Tottenham way, isn't a good idea, trust me. So all they got for their troubles was to get whacked about by the riot police, get themselves a massive escort, which in turn meant they would be safe as houses, but could give it all the big one from the safety of their escort. You probably had every barman, waitress and toilet cleaner in London. So their actual firm was probably about 200-strong. There were a lot who had foolishly strayed from the escort, which resulted in a few of their bods face-down on the pavement unconscious.

In the ground, there were pockets of the cunts everywhere. And where they could get reached they were getting battered every time they stood up, except in the West Stand, where the directors' boxes and so forth are situated, where they are more likely to get clapped than clumped by the silly bastards. But the general opinion from the boys was that they weren't impressed by the way they wasted such a massive turnout. With those numbers, they should have been down the Lane all afternoon, not hiding behind a police escort.

231

Mind you, personally, I would give them some credit for at least putting on a bit of a show, which is a lot more than a lot of teams do down the Lane.

On the pitch Spurs secured a 2–1 win by the skin of their teeth, which wasn't enough to lift the gloom hanging over the Lane under Ramos and his fellow clowns.

SECOND LEG

I'm not going to waste much time on this leg as it surprisingly isn't worth it. This was the leg that everyone was looking forward to: the Poles in their own manor.

All sorts of scenarios were to be expected. A bloodbath was predicted: running battles in the park with baseball bats, which was supposedly their little trick. Well, whatever the Poles had, they left it at the Lane. I was obviously right when I said that every fucking Pole is over here, because none of the mugs was over there.

And don't believe all that bollocks when you see pictures of them all queuing up at Victoria coach station waiting for the bus home. That's just Labour propaganda.

Anyway, our firm were wrapped up by the Old Bill and they were nowhere to be seen. So, all in all, a total fucking waste of time. Spurs scraped through a dismal game on aggregate, which put us into the draw for the group stages.

CHAPTER 15
SUMMING UP

What can I say? This book has been a nightmare to do from start to finish for all sorts of reasons, which could be another book in itself. I'm sure that, as time passes, I will be proud of this book as I was of the first, *Tottenham Massive*. I had heard it was harder to make a second book, but I didn't think it would be true. Yet it is, and it was. It probably doesn't help when I get fucked off with myself to say the least.

I went to Trooping of the Colour one Saturday with the women in my life: my little one, my missus and my mum. We were treated like royalty itself and I would like to thank the Scots Guards, the Irish Guards and the Grenadier Guards for their hospitality back at their camp. My little girl loved it, and she was very lucky to see it at

233

her age. In fact, we all were. There is normally a four-year waiting list, but my pal is a captain in the Scots Guards. He got us tickets in the same block as that pig Gordon Brown. It is a great day, though, and it is true that you cannot get an idea of what it is like unless you are there, when all the horses, the gun carriages and the cavalry come out of Green Park to line up in their gleaming plumes behind the troops themselves. It's a sight for sore eyes, believe me. You could actually picture the scene hundreds of years back on some foreign field as they are flying into battle.

Unfortunately, the day went on too long, and I should've gone with my gut instinct and left with my missus. After a few hours of silly amounts of booze, I knew it would go pear-shaped; these things always do. And it didn't help that I was shattered, as I had been doing a variety of jobs to keep the wolf from the door.

It didn't help that I was tired from the night before and then had to stand in agony for hours in these stupid fucking pointy brown shoes I had bought. After leaving the house I realised they were killing me. I should've said fuck it to the bar after, but, once again, I put myself out for other people, which is wrong. I wisely sent my little girl home at 6pm, but I carried on. I knew it was a mistake, but there you go.

To cut a long story short, it was too much booze, not enough food, being hot and tired, you name it. I was not happy the way things turned out and I put myself in a really vulnerable situation getting so pissed. But I thought I could let my guard down for the night and I nearly came unstuck. Something I won't do again, which is quite sad, really.

OLD LONDON TOWN

I've had two major setbacks recently. One was when a floppy disk broke – 10,000 words and weeks of work just gone. Just now my fucking piece-of-shit computer has gone on me again; I can't believe it. It's just a head fuck. It doesn't help that my computer would be out of date in the History Museum and, whatever happens, I'm throwing it straight out once this nightmare is over.

London. My home town. What can I say? I was going to dedicate a whole chapter to the feral scum who roam the streets of the city without a care in the world by all accounts, but they're just not worth it. It's happy days except for the old boys and girls who are too scared to go outside the front door after three in the afternoon.

Why don't they just ban hoods? What the fuck have the silly cunts got to hide? They know what they are doing, so fuck them and just ban them. The Old Bill are quick enough to come down on our lot like a ton of bricks, but they let these tramps run free. It is fucking wrong and the Old Bill know it.

The thing that makes me laugh is that they must stink,

have bad haircuts or both. London is a melting pot and people who want to play by the rules are welcome. I have friends from every corner of the globe and they are sickened, just like me, at the way things are going in the city. And the politicians wonder why the British National Party is getting so strong. Wake up before it's too late!

As I said, everything has gone wrong with this book and there came a stage where I thought, Fuck this! I don't need this, I really don't – from being fucked around by pricks from Barnsley who aren't fit to lace your boots to the broken disk, which really fucked me off and put me off my game big time. My pal Kal, who has done this computer work, has been a godsend.

Last time I did this kind of work I kept it simple. I wrote it down and then got it typed up. Very old school, I know, but it worked. This time I have written it, typed some of it and not known if I was coming or going – it just scrambles your mind. Combine that with trying to keep a long-distance relationship going…

I think you get the drift. It made me quite depressed, really. Anyone who has written a book will understand me; those who haven't will think I'm acting like a prick. Don't get me wrong: I'm not asking for sympathy; I knew what I was getting myself into. Like everyone, you just want a fair crack at the whip. I know that once this comes out I will get all the silly calls and threats; but when it gets personal, and other people just judge you on what they hear about you, well it's just fucking sad and petty and obviously jealousy. But you can't get that through to your nearest and dearest, as they think you're just getting yourself at it.

I think you know by now where the worst place for that is. When things really start to get me down, though, the fighter in me kicks in and I think of the privileged position that I am in, that I have this opportunity to write another book. People may not like what it is about, but a book is a book, and all books require a similar amount of sacrifice on the part of the author.

It has been hard being away from the boys because of the banning orders and court cases and so forth. Even though it will always be in my blood, you just can't stand still.

UNFINISHED BUSINESS

Our firm is now the best in the country, that's for sure. How long for? Well, that is the million-dollar question and it comes down to how much the boys want it. The yoof are phenomenal and backed up by a few boys who never seem to age; they are pretty much untouchable on their day. Am I going to call it a day? I don't think so. I have too much unfinished business to deal with. Maybe one more season, just for luck. What do you think? I wouldn't tell you, or the Old Bill, in any case. All in all, I haven't regretted any of it. How could I? I just wish people wouldn't judge you without knowing you (you know who you are!).

On a lighter note, it has been a real buzz having people coming up and asking me to sign books for them in the street or wherever. Would have been nice if a few more girls had been asking, though, and I don't mean that in a big-headed way. It's just nice to have people being appreciative of your work. (Sound like a fucking writer now, don't I?)

One of the best examples of that is when I was sitting outside the Drift bar in Southsea one lovely sunny day last year with my pal Andy. This geezer kept crisscrossing the road in front of us. I was thinking, What the fuck is *that* all about? Now my pal is a big lump to say the least, and a former Royal Marine, and he was getting uneasy in his seat when this fella came up to me and asked if I was Trevor Tanner and asked if I could sign his book. Thank fuck! I thought. I was only too happy to oblige. Nice to see some Spurs in Pompey, anyway.

But my pal's face was a picture. We have a standing joke that he thinks I set it up, and have the geezer continually walking around (good idea, though). Of course, I had never seen the geezer in my life. My pal just got the hump because I was asked for my autograph outside his boozer. Typical Pompey (only joking, broth). We still laugh about it today; things like that are all good fun.

Another time I was followed into Thornton's in the West End when I was buying an Easter egg for my little one and my missus. Again, all good, but I'm not sure who was more shocked, me or the bird behind the counter.

As you may know, I did a TV programme called *The Real Football Factories* with Danny Dyer on Bravo TV, and I've heard all sorts of shit saying that I had a pop at him, and he has been saying I was a nightmare to interview on the Internet. I hate the fucking Internet – all that chatroom bollocks – and I think it is dangerous stuff to mess around with. Full of weirdos and snidey cunts who haven't got the bottle to chat up a bird in real life or say what they think to someone's face, or in person (got that off my chest).

Anyway, Dyer is entitled to his opinion. The only thing I got the hump about was that he didn't stay behind with the boys for a drink afterwards. I stand by what I said about his film *The Real Football Factories*, though. I thought it was shit, but, then again, most of those films are, with the same faces popping up every two minutes. They are just boring and untrue, as they never give us the credit we are due.

IN SAFE HANDS

On the playing side Spurs are in good hands with Harry Redknapp, as long as the chairman Levy keeps out of it. I can see us going from strength to strength, as long as

Harry doesn't get nicked. He just happens to have pissed off the whole of Pompey in the meantime (oh, well). The new fixtures have come out frighteningly quickly as I write this, and I see that we have the Scousers first game of the season and Chelsea nice and early. Will I be there? What do *you* think? And of course this book will hit the streets just in time for the next World Cup in 2010. Happy days!

How will we get on? I'm not saying a thing. How South Africa got to host it is anyone's guess and obviously political. And no doubt England will be out there in their thousands and Spurs will have one of the biggest followings out there, as they did in the last tournaments. We were at all the ones I was fucking banned from. You never know: you might see me there. I really fancy it this season. Hopefully, I'm off to Portugal with my missus to burn my other leg this summer. Either that or check into a nuthouse. So have fun, people, because it's all a game really. To absent friends at Her Majesty's pleasure: Martin, Johnny, Terry. You will all be out when this hits the streets (that's something to look forward to).

To everyone who has backed me in my personal life or helped me directly in whatever way with this book, thank you from the bottom of my heart.

For all the doubters and haters, fuck you.

TOTTENHAM MASSIVE

Trevor Tanner

Trevor Tanner headed the Tottenham Massive for 15 years. He's still doing it. So it is only fitting that the main man himself is finally setting the record straight about the truth of Spurs' formidable reputation. This compelling book shows how the Massive forced just about everyone to sit up and take notice of them.

Tanner's first-hand accounts tell of the long ride to the top, including the brutal ten-year war with hated rivals Chelsea. His focus and dedication to his firm has meant he has often clashed with the law, accumulating numerous convictions respect for the firm has often been at the expense of his own freedom – resulting in him spending three years in prison.

Indeed, the price paid for such a long struggle has often been very personal. Among the hardest battles of all has been tat of securing custody of his beloved daughter. This is the story of a man who doesn't compromise and a firm that takes no prisoners.

ISBN 978-1-84454-351-9

John Blake Publishing Ltd

OUT NOW

TO ORDER SIMPLY CALL THIS NUMBER
+ 44 (0) 207 381 0666

Or visit our website www.johnblakepublishing.co.uk

Free P+P and UK Delivery
(Abroad £3.00 per book)

Prices and availability subject to change without notice